SIR, I HAVE A PROBLEM

R. LOFTON HUDSON

Sir, I Have a Problem

THOMAS Y. CROWELL COMPANY

NEW YORK

Established 1834

❧ PREFACE

WHEN PEOPLE ARE IN TROUBLE they need help in a hurry. It is quite a commentary on our culture that people have to write letters to someone whom they have never seen and about whom they know little. They are seeking someone who will take their problems seriously. This I have always done. And it has been a most enjoyable, though at times frightening, responsibility.

Some of the letters make me feel like catching the next plane in order to help the individual involved. "I have no one to turn to" is a frequent sentence in these letters. Many of them, however, are from people who say, "Your answer this week fits my case perfectly . . . thank you."

The questions and answers in this volume are from a column I write for several weekly religious periodicals, which total over a million circulation. It is called "Counselor's Corner." Editors are very generous in reporting that many readers turn to this column first when they get the mail. If some people are helped, or even entertained, I am grateful.

Some arrogance and presumption have no doubt crept into these answers. Usually readers have written to correct me. For most of these comments I have been grateful, too.

R. LOFTON HUDSON

v

❧ CONTENTS

EMOTIONAL PROBLEMS

Christians Can Become Mentally Ill	1
Roommate Acts Funny	2
Depressed Sunday School Teacher	3
Brother in Mental Hospital	4
Made Mess of Life	5
Mother Still Grieving	6
Grieving Wife	7
Fussy Father	8
Hush-Hush About Mental Illness	9
Helping the Alcoholic	10
Alcoholic Husband	11
Chronic Worrier	12
Allergies	13
Positive Thinking Cult	14
Worry Over Old Sin	15
My Bad Temper	16
Afraid of Lightning	17
Unconscious Wish for Death	18
Premonition of Death	19
Stage Fright	20
Guilt Toward Parents	21

My Late Wife   22
Wife Loves Another Man   23
Loveless Marriage   24
Husband's Parents   25
Dogs Ahead of Family   26
No Longer in Love   27
Called But Cranky   28
Husband Wants Divorce   29
Home Breaking Up   30
Prodigal Husband   31
Ex-Wife Threatens   32
A "Mean Woman"   33
Mad Husband   34
Grouchy Husband   35
Preacher's Wife   36
Coaxing a Husband   37
Unloved Husband   38
Divorce May Be Criminal   39
Unhappy Woman   40
Jealous Wife   41
Wife Confesses   42
Don't Run Away   43
Should Husband Apologize?   44
Prodigal Husband Returns   45
Should a Wife Forgive?   46
Is Husband to Boss Wife?   47
Obedience of Wives Again   48
Calls Church Unprintable Names   49

OTHER FAMILY PROBLEMS

Mother-in-Law Hate   50
Mother-in-Law Trouble   51
Son-in-Law Trouble   52

In-Law Trouble   53
Illegitimate Parents   54
Sisters Quarrel   55
Can't Stand Children   56
Hateful Sister   57
Frightened Children   58
Boy Who Steals   59
Have Mercy on My Son   60
Homosexual Boy   61
Domineering Father   62
Family Altar Problem   63
Middle-Age Delinquency   64

LOVE AND COURTSHIP

Eager Spinsters   65
No Good as Husband   66
Prospective Husband   67
Uncertain Bridegroom   68
Woman's College Girl   69
Prodigal Son   70
He Loves Me?   71
On Marrying Divorcees   72
Dominating Mother   73
Love by Mail   74
Girl Friend Drinks   75
Confessing Past Sins   76
Not in Love   77

RIGHT OR WRONG?

Can a Christian Be a Movie Actor?   78
Teen-Age Problem   79
Teen-Agers' Dress   80
Sons of Ham   81
Divorced Couple   82
Chain Letters   83

The Christian Sabbath   84
Picture Shows   85
Country Clubbers   86
Insane Husband   87
Beating School Children   88
Capital Punishment   89
Segregation   90
Christian Lawsuits   91

WHAT DOES THE BIBLE SAY?

Baseball at Church   93
Ping-Pong at Church   94
Divorced Christian   95
Unequally Yoked   96
Loving Enemies   97
Where We Go When We Die   98
Are Infants Saved?   99
Unpardonable Sin   100
Prosperous Sinners   101
State of the Heathen   102
Chronic Doubter   103
Daughter's Clothes   104
Suicides   105
Evolution   106
Are Jews God's Favorites?   108

CHURCH PROBLEMS

Church Picture Stolen   109
Tithing Problem   110
Women in the Church   111
Bad Housekeeping   112
Money for All Causes   113
Nominating Committee Unkind   114
"Shelved" Members   115

Too Sick to Fight   116
New Version   117
Pastor Won't Pay Bills   118
Choir Members   119
Using First Names   120
Can't Go to Church   121
Blames Preacher for Marriage   122
Deacon's Wife   123
Treasurer Refuses   124
Scared Church Member   125
Pagan Christmas   126
Santa Claus   127
Happy Young People   128
Baptist Bridge   129
Song-Title Sermons   130
Clique in Church   131
Anonymous Letters   132

RELIGIOUS PROBLEMS

Why So Critical?   133
When Converted   134
Forgiving Enemy   135
Plagued by Doubts   136
Answering God's Call   137
Seduced by Church Worker   138
Judged by Heart or Mind?   139
Tempted to Sin   140
Cruel Criticism   141
Bad Disease Problem   142
Billy Graham Revivals   143
Join the Human Race   144

INDEX   145

INDEX OF SCRIPTURE PASSAGES   147

❧ EMOTIONAL PROBLEMS

Christians Can Become Mentally Ill

QUESTION: *My pastor preaches that if a person would give his heart to Christ and live for Christ, he would not need to go to a psychiatrist. He also says that a real Christian would never commit suicide.*

Is this true? I have known some good Christians who got sick mentally.

ANSWER: It is true that if an individual were reared from infancy in an atmosphere of Christian love and, when he is old enough, became a dedicated Christian and lived as one all his life, he would *probably* never need the services of a psychiatrist. But who has? Sin may lead to emotional illness in that it leads to confusion and frustration.

But some of the finest Christians I know have needed the services of psychiatrists. Brain tumors, toxic conditions, hardening of the arteries, and many other physical difficulties may cause insane reactions. And many converted people were injured emotionally in childhood and will get sick even if they trust in the Lord for salvation.

Your pastor is entirely wrong about suicides. Most suicides are ill mentally and could be treated if our society did not consider depressions and anxiety a disgrace and a sin. Your pastor is probably sincere, and he is right in emphasizing the importance of religion to mental health. But, actually, he is helping the suicide rate by such preaching. Three of the finest ministers I have known have committed suicide within the last few years.

Religion does not claim to cure mumps, scabies, polio, or diabetes. Why should it discourage treatment for people with delusions, or depressed people, or those who have abnormal fears?

Roommate Acts Funny

QUESTION: *I am a business girl and have recently acquired a new roommate. She told me that she had spent some time in a mental hospital and was still under the care of a doctor. Lately she has been talking to some imaginary person in the room, gets very nervous, and looks funny at times. I am not afraid of her, but what I want to know is how to help her. Can you tell me?*

ANSWER: If you are not afraid of your roommate you are very fortunate. That in itself will help. What emotionally sick people need is to be surrounded by secure friends. You have a chance of a lifetime to show some real Christian love. You can help a great deal. Just be natural and kind. Never criticize nor blame. If she says nothing to you about any other person in the room, just act as if nothing has happened. Whatever you do, do not reprimand her nor try to talk her out of her behavior. Leave that to the doctor.

The one ironclad rule for helping such people is honesty. If they find a person who is dishonest with them, it disturbs them more than you can imagine. They simply do

2

not know what the real world is like. When she says, "Do you hear the voices?" just answer her calmly, "No, I did not hear a thing." Be honest at all times.

Act normally and naturally if you want to help. Be friendly, kind, and encouraging. If associates will simply treat these people as if they are valuable, good, lovable people—and not blame them nor try to analyze them—they will often work out their own problems. If your roommate gets worse, call her doctor.

Depressed Sunday School Teacher

QUESTION: *I am sixty-eight years old and have been an active church member for fifty years. I have taught a men's class in the Sunday school for years before my retirement and have served as deacon.*

Now I am depressed. I feel that I want to die. I know this is wrong, but no one seems to be able to tell me what to do. My doctor just laughs at me and tells me that I will feel better before long, but I don't. If I were a good Christian, couldn't I throw this off?

ANSWER: I can imagine how you feel. It is not too uncommon for people your age to be depressed. You feel inadequate and worthless and even guilty.

Depression is anger at self. It comes from a severe conscience, and is a very untrustworthy feeling. No, you are probably depressed because you are a good Christian rather than the other way round. Your standards are high, and now you feel guilty because you can't achieve as much as you did formerly.

First, don't blame yourself because you want to die. To

blame yourself simply adds to your load. Second, watch yourself to see what causes you to be irritated or to feel anxious, and avoid it like the measles. Be good to yourself. Third, play something. Dominoes, cards, checkers, put jigsaw puzzles together—anything that you can do with your hands and that is pure play. Last, when you pray, pray calm prayers and know that even though God seems a million miles away, He hears every word you say, and cares.

Brother in Mental Hospital

QUESTION: *I have a brother who is now in our state mental hospital. He is twenty-seven years old and in the past five years has been in this institution over half of the time. He has used liquor excessively, doped, and gambled. The folks thought that he must be insane and put him in the hospital. He has been given all sorts of treatment but each time he is released, he starts running around again. For the past eight months he has not been given any treatments, but the doctors say that he is not ready to get out. They call him a psychopathic patient. If you know anything about them, I would appreciate hearing from you.*

ANSWER: The psychopathic personalities are those who "act out their primitive impulses without regard to the rules and regulations laid down by society"—or for that matter, God. They are not insane (or psychotic) and some authorities do not consider them neurotic. They often come from good homes, and are usually very bright, attractive people. They are morally deformed or twisted and are extremely difficult to help. Few of them are ever cured, and when they are, it is usually necessary to have them under controlled conditions, such as in a hospital.

Unless your brother can be treated successfully, which is unlikely, it will be best for him and for society if he can remain in a hospital the remainder of his life. Otherwise he will be in and out of jails.

The hospital is probably doing what they can for your brother. Shock treatments and the like do not help in such cases. Stand by the doctors and don't take your brother out until they advise it.

Made Mess of Life

QUESTION: *I am writing to you for advice. Maybe I want sympathy, but I need help.*

I have made a mess of my life. Through my own fault (and sins) my marriage has gone on the rocks. I have repented of this and have told my pastor of my intention to do better, but my wife has left me, and I am out of a job—due to drink and sin. I wonder if it is worth trying again.

ANSWER: My dear sir, the church has been salvaging people like you for 1900 years. If you have come clean with Christ and have realized that God gives you another chance, you are well on the road to recovery.

If I were you, I think I would go to church every time the doors are open. If they need someone to sweep the floors, turn out the lights, ring the bells, carry flowers to the sick, you will be the one to volunteer. Great Christians are made out of people like you. The Holy Spirit will lead you in every step of the way. Learn to take orders. God does not want you to spend the rest of your life beating and blaming yourself. Serve. Love. Devote yourself to the kingdom of God. You may be a success in God's sight yet. God's grace is really demonstrated in people like you.

Mother Still Grieving

QUESTION: *My mother is making a poor adjustment to my father's death. She doesn't want to be alone at any time. When I am dressing for a date, she begins to sniffle about being all alone. This is making me miserable. I cannot stay at home with her all of the time, even if she does cry. And I cannot take her with me. How long does it take a person to get over this? And what can I do to help her?*

ANSWER: If your father has been dead for as much as six months to a year, I would say that your mother needs the help of a trained counselor. Grief situations often lead to chronic maladjustments.

No, I would not stay at home all of the time. Neither would I be harsh and unkind to my mother. She is sick, emotionally and spiritually. The best thing to remember is to be kind and firm with her. When she tells you how pathetic her situation is, say, "Yes, I know you feel that way. I hope you can find some way to overcome that feeling." It does no good to blame, and usually little good to advise. Just drop a suggestion here and there. Take your mother to church. She may hear a sermon that will challenge her to move on in life.

No one can tell you how soon she may get over her withdrawal from life. But if you let her dominate you by her illness, you will develop a deep hostility toward her. So don't blame yourself as a daughter. Just live a normal life and trust God for the future.

Grieving Wife

QUESTION: *Four months ago my husband, forty-two years of age, was taken away from me by a heart attack.*

Now I cannot pray, I do not care whether I go to church or meet people, and I even resent having to do things for my two children. Will I ever get over this? I was not like this before.

ANSWER: Don't be ashamed of your wayward emotions. When people are in grief, they are often angry and unmotivated. Their wheels spin. No one seems to understand them, and most of the time the grieving person does not care what others think.

After four months you should begin to move on in life. However, sometimes it takes much longer. Every person must solve his grief problem in his own way and at his own speed.

Now about your praying and your churchgoing. Keep putting one foot in front of the other and doing the best you can. Tell God how you feel and know that He understands your crazy emotions. He loves you even if you cannot love Him.

If you don't feel better soon, go to your pastor or to some Christian leader and pour out your heart. Yes, you will finally win, if you grow. No one can do as much for you as the Lord can. He will help you as you decide to quit fighting Him.

Fussy Father

QUESTION: *My father is an invalid and he says that he is a Christian, but every time something doesn't go his way, he gets mad and takes his spite out on one of the family. He gets terribly mad and says terrible things. I am afraid one of us will have a nervous breakdown.*

Is there anything I could do to help him or stop him from doing this way? This is serious. It is so hard to be a Christian under such circumstances.

ANSWER: There is always a Christian approach to any problem. I can imagine how serious your problem is.

Treat your father as a patient. Do not cross him any oftener than you have to. Do not make him feel guilty. And encourage him to see people. Be firm and kind.

Many people, as they get older, are cranky and crabbed. They are angry. Besides the fact that age brings certain deprivations and frustrations, the arteries begin to harden and their rational controls are not so good. If we live long enough, most of us will get that way. It is hard to be an invalid. Put yourself in his place.

If your father has ever been a Christian, he still is. Our heavenly Father understands him and loves him.

Don't have a nervous breakdown. Respect yourself, even if you do feel hostile toward your father. Nervous breakdowns usually grow out of loss of self-esteem. God loves us. Let's love ourselves.

Hush-Hush About Mental Illness

QUESTION: *My sister is in a mental hospital and has been for ten years. All of the family is hush-hush about the whole matter, and I think they are wrong. It seems to me that mental illness is no more a disgrace than physical. What do you think about this? Should I go along with the family and try to keep my sister's illness a secret?*

ANSWER: You are exactly right. Good people often get sick emotionally. And it is nothing to be ashamed of.

If you are a Christian, you should do everything you can to overcome this idea that emotionally sick people are to blame, or are weak or sinful. Visit your sister if the hospital advises it. Act toward her as you would toward anyone else. Love her. That is what she needs.

Of course, as long as there is so much stupidity and misinformation about emotional disorders, it does no good to advertise that a person has been sick that way. Perhaps you can reason with the family.

Then, if you can't help your family, you may help others. In most communities there are some alert, informed people. Join them. And try to talk down the "disgrace" angle in mental illness. There should be no more blame attached to a stay in a mental hospital than in a tuberculosis hospital.

Helping the Alcoholic

QUESTION: *My husband is an alcoholic. He has been drinking for fifteen years. Twice he has been baptized and has seemed to rededicate his life, but he was not able to hold out.*

What can I do? He will not go to see a psychiatrist and he won't go to Alcoholics Anonymous. Do these hospitals that claim "cures" really help?

ANSWER: How do you know that your husband is an alcoholic? Only a person with a great deal of knowledge of alcoholism can recognize an alcoholic. Many excessive drinkers are not alcoholics. And some alcoholics have other emotional disorders which need to be treated also. Read Marty Mann's *Primer on Alcoholism* (Rinehart); or better still, Clifford J. Earle's *How to Help an Alcoholic* (Westminster); and later, Howard J. Clinebell's *Understanding and Counseling the Alcoholic* (Abingdon). Ask your bookstore or library.

Frankly, I believe that it would be more easy to tell you what not to do. Don't lecture him. It does no good and probably prolongs his immaturity. Second, don't pull his chestnuts out of the fire. Usually it is impossible to help an alcoholic if somebody, especially a member of the family, will get him out of a jam every time he gets into one. All you can do is to protect yourself and wait and keep praying.

No, hospitals are usually not the answer for excessive drinkers, even for alcoholics. They can dry them up, but what is to keep them from getting drunk again?

Alcoholic Husband

QUESTION: *I married a drunkard but, honest, I didn't know he was a drunkard until after I had married him. Now after twenty-two years we have a darling son, twenty-one, and a daughter, nineteen. They have finished school by us living in torment to do it, and now have good jobs. He gets drunk two or three times a week and curses me and threatens to beat me. Sometimes I have to leave home and am afraid to come back. It is ruining my nerves. His daddy did his mother that same way.*

Should I go on like this the rest of my life?

ANSWER: I don't think so. However, you will miss him if you leave him. Nearly every woman who marries an alcoholic man has an unconscious desire to be punished. They take years of punishment because it is their way of relieving themselves of guilt feeling. Then as soon as they divorce one alcoholic, they (unconsciously) seek out another and marry him. This may sound silly to you, but it is so.

I think you have a personal problem to be solved, which divorce will not solve. How does it happen that you put up with all of this cruelty? Surely you do not think that it is helping him, and it hardly seems that God would require you to accept such injustice.

Try Alcoholics Anonymous. Try getting him to church and Sunday school. Try everything. If these do not work, see a lawyer. But don't see a lawyer until you mean business. Then make it stick. Drop him like a hot potato. If this does not bring him to seek a cure, there is no hope.

Chronic Worrier

QUESTION: *My trouble is worry. In addition, I have stomach trouble and severe headaches (but not migraine). I have spells when I can't sleep and when I get up more tired than when I went to bed.*

My husband says that all my troubles are in my mind. My doctor says that there is nothing physically wrong with me. My mother tells me that I am just being silly; and my children don't know what to think.

ANSWER: The world's work is done by people somewhat like yourself. You worry? Who doesn't, if he is "right bright"? You can't sleep at times? Most people have spells of insomnia. Perhaps your physical symptoms are serving you a good purpose and warding off some more serious and destructive manner of handling anxiety.

Don't let anyone shame you about your troubles by telling you that they are imaginary. If you feel bad, you feel bad, whether the cause is chemical or emotional. And, of course, what your doctor means is that he cannot find any organic difficulty. He does not mean that you are functioning well physically.

If you cannot find some intelligent counselor to talk your problems out with, you might just as well learn to bear them nobly and not yell too much about them. But do not be ashamed of them. You may develop what one of my friends calls "frantic serenity."

Allergies

QUESTION: *I have allergies, food allergies. In fact there are only a few foods that I can eat without a stomach and intestinal upset. My boss laughs at me and says that it is all in my mind. He is a Christian Scientist and urges me to go to a reader. He says that my trouble is negative thinking. What do you think?*

ANSWER: I think "negative" about your boss. His attitude seems to me to be positively unscientific. Furthermore, it is thoroughly unchristian to act as if illness is a person's own fault. I am sure that Christian Scientists do a lot of good, but if they could cure allergies, the world would make a path to their door.

There are some allergies which are apparently hysterical symptoms. That is, they are caused by anxiety; the fearful person runs to his body for help. Any of the faith healers can cure some of these sufferers of their particular difficulty. But they may switch symptoms or even be worse off emotionally after they are "cured." And, of course, some allergic conditions clear up for no reason at all, so far as the doctors can find out.

If I were you, I would go to a good allergy specialist and follow his advice. Then pray for God's help and healing. If God wills to heal you, he will; He is no respecter of persons. But do not let anybody fool you on this "positive thinking" stuff. It is not the solution to all of man's problems. The only kind of thinking which honors God and respects intelligence is realistic, honest, straight thinking.

Positive Thinking Cult

QUESTION: *Your comments on "negative thinking" and on faith healing make me wonder if you have become acquainted with the field of psychosomatic medicine. And do you know about the many people today who are doing faith healing?*

I do not understand why my own denomination does not go in for divine healing. Others do. Can you tell me?

ANSWER: I cannot speak for any one denomination, but I imagine most of them believe, as I do, that God can heal, and that we ought to pray for healing. But professional faith healing is a different thing. Most of it is just plain quackery. I have personally known several people, who are now dead, who might have been alive if they had turned to a physician for proper diagnosis and treatment. This is especially true of cancer and heart cases. Furthermore, many people who claim faith healing have simply switched symptoms. They are still disturbed people, and some of them are physically ill. I believe in medicine *and* faith. Not either-or.

If you think that the new field of psychosomatic medicine claims that all illnesses are due to "negative thinking," you are wrong. It simply recognizes that the emotions can make the body sick and that the mind needs to be treated accordingly.

The "positive thinking" cult is very widespread today. It does not cure, although I am sure that it does some good. It does not get rid of the causes of illness, but it may help the individual to select the focus of his thought. Imagine Paul or Jesus telling someone to "think positively." I am glad for an example of true divine healing, but God does not honor those who reject his true Gospel. This is Satan's method of misleading the unsuspecting.

Worry Over Old Sin

QUESTION: *I am heartsick over something that happened to me over twenty-five years ago. I got in with the wrong crowd and had an awful downfall. I got out of their company and repented of my sins and have worked in the church ever since. God has blessed me with a fine son and daughter and now a grandchild. Often I feel happy in church but then the old feelings of shame come back. Why can't I forget, if I have been forgiven?*

ANSWER: You are suffering from an emotional trouble known as melancholia or depression. Often a depressed person will rake his memories to find old sins to talk about, or inquire about the unpardonable sin, or say he feels that he is lost and cannot be saved. From fifteen to twenty thousand such people commit suicide every year in the United States.

The general public often turns a deaf ear to the cries of such depressed people, or quotes them a verse of Scripture, or tells them "not to be silly." But it takes more than that to cure a depression.

The reason you are bringing up your old sin is to tantalize yourself because you feel that you ought to be punished. Actually depression is anger at self. You are angry because you feel that you are not loved.

God loves you. People will love you if you will let them. Don't give up hope. Soften your severe conscience if you can. And if you do not get better, see a medical doctor. When people worry over sins committed long ago, they are sick, not merely heartsick.

My Bad Temper

QUESTION: *I have an uncontrollable temper. From childhood (I am now thirty-three) I have been like this. When someone says something which makes me mad, I simply blow up. I get red in the face and say things for which I am ashamed in five minutes. My wife says that it is the devil in me, and I just about believe her. But what I want to know is what I can do about it. I have prayed. I read the Bible. I even apologize for what I have said, but somehow I don't get rid of it.*

ANSWER: Perhaps your wife is right about it's being the devil in you. At least the Old Fellow is using this to cripple you as a Christian. Have you ever thought why you get so mad? Anger is the way children defend themselves, and it works, or did when they were little. At least, it seemed to. But now that you are grown, there are better ways of meeting opposition. Some sulk, or get very quiet, even deny that they feel anything, but they do.

I would suggest that you sit down and think over the last ten times you have blown up. You will find a pattern that runs through all of them. There are one or more points at which you feel terribly weak and inferior. Your anger is nothing but a defense of some sort, and it is a dead giveaway. You are actually confessing to the world how insecure and uncertain you are.

There is a place for anger—in resisting oppression—but

you are overdoing it (Eph. 4:26). It is, however, a very dangerous emotion (Matt. 5:22). Even Jesus showed anger once (Mark 3:5), but it was coupled with grief. You can overcome the worst of a bad temper if you will grow up (1 Cor. 13:11).

Afraid of Lightning

QUESTION: *I am deathly afraid of lightning. Of course, there are many things that frighten me at times, but I always pray over them and find a solution. I feel so ashamed over this fear. It seems that each time I get so afraid over lightning it shuts His presence away from me. My friends all laugh at me. I don't think they mean to be cruel. It does seem foolish, but I cannot overcome it. I even get violently sick at my stomach.*

Do you think something is wrong with my faith? Or could it be a nervous disorder?

ANSWER: Your friends are wrong. Such fears are not funny. Nor are they due to a lack of faith. They can't be cured by prayer or "positive thinking" or by any mental tricks. Prayer will help, if you pray right. And faith will steady you and give you courage.

Of course, such abnormal fear is a nervous disorder. To speak of it as an "emotional disorder" is probably a little more accurate. It might even be thought of as an illness of the unconscious. But you cannot overcome it by conscious effort, and religion aims at the conscious.

Personally, I am deathly afraid of high places. Most people have some kind of phobia. I am living with mine—and staying away from high places.

Your fear of lightning might be removed by an expert psychotherapist—if you are young, have plenty of money, and will take two or three years in the process. Otherwise manage your fear the best you can and quit being ashamed of it. God does not hold you responsible for something you cannot help.

Unconscious Wish for Death

QUESTION: *Since my two-months-old baby was found dead in bed, I have frequently had screaming spells, saying to my husband, "Don't let me die; please don't let me die." I feel that I am losing my mind. I have horrible dreams of murder, cancer, and all forms of death. What can I do? I pray, read my Bible, and am active in every phase of church work, but these do not seem to help.*

ANSWER: It sounds to me as if you have an unconscious wish to die. Many people do. There seems to be in every human being a kind of automatic justice-maker—a conscience, we call it. If we have violated our consciences and not admitted it frankly, then the "sentence" or punishment must be worked out secretly. Perhaps you feel that your neglect caused the child's death.

You may have wished that the little one would die, and quickly repressed it. Or you may be punishing your husband by making him listen to you scream. You may even be holding this fear of death before your eyes to keep you from doing something you have an urge to do that you consider wrong. The human mind is very complex.

If you had a kidney trouble you would go to a urologist. For heart trouble you go to a cardiac specialist. Why don't you insist on your doctor referring you to a psychiatrist, who specializes in emotional disturbances?

Premonition of Death

QUESTION: *When I was about twelve years of age I began wondering if I would live to be sixteen, and thought I would die before then. I finished high school and entered nurses' training, but that fear still persists. Now I am twenty-three and my fear is that I will not live to be thirty.*

What I'd like to know, do you think it is a premonition that I will die young or just a phobia? I have thought that it could be something that happened in my childhood, but as I look back I can't find anything.

ANSWER: Of course you cannot remember anything that may have caused your fear. In fact, there may not be any one thing. If there were, you would not likely turn it up like a mouse out of a new-plowed furrow. Psychotherapy is a slow, painful process.

Your problem is an overdeveloped conscience. This may sound strange, but some people's consciences get all twisted and enlarged and corrupted. Some have too much conscience; some too little. The Apostle Paul is enough to prove that consciences are not, by themselves, trustworthy. He persecuted the church "in all good conscience."

Premonitions are usually a kind of superstition. Perhaps they always are, but I know that they are usually. We quickly forget the ones that do not come true.

No, you expect to die because you have repressed some guilt feelings. If you cannot forget your fears, see some good counselor. My guess is that you will live to be at least eighty.

Stage Fright

QUESTION: *I would like to ask how to control your fear when you are called on to pray or speak. It seems that my mind becomes a complete blank, and I can't think. I have been an active member of the church for three years and teach in the Intermediate Department and am church clerk. This awful fear keeps me from doing my best. Can you offer suggestions?*

ANSWER: In a way you ought to thank God for your fear. It keeps you from making a fool of yourself. Besides, it proves that you are a good man who cares what people think of you, even if you care a little too much.

Here are my suggestions: First, do not quit doing your best, even though you never get over your fear. Just don't let your fears work. Keep on shaking if you must, but do not quit speaking.

Second, do not be ashamed of your fears. Most other people have some of the same fear when they speak in public. I know that the Bible says, "Fear not," but Jesus also said, "I will forewarn you whom ye shall fear" (Luke 12:5). Fear of that which is dangerous is natural and good.

Third, stage fright is fear of rejection or of criticism. You are afraid of losing face, afraid of what some cad will say. Be humble. God will help people to accept you as you are. Risk their love. Those who can will love you, and that will be enough to make you fairly comfortable. After all, you don't have to be Demosthenes. Be yourself.

Finally, pray and thank God for his help. Quote to yourself His blessed promises. Then shake if you must, but do your duty in Christ's name.

Guilt Toward Parents

QUESTION: *I married without my parents' consent at the age of eighteen, seven years ago. We now have two fine children, and my parents say that they have forgiven me, but for some reason I still feel guilty and don't seem to be able to stop it. I deceived my parents and hurt them deeply. What can I do to overcome this feeling?*

ANSWER: It occurs to me that you are worrying about something that you did not even mention in your letter. I have seen many such cases as yours and helped them work through their real guilt feelings. This does not mean that I can guess what your real worry is. I cannot. But your worries are irrational.

My guess is that you are a very conscientious person who wants to love everybody and thinks everybody ought to love you. Sister, that is not the way the world is made. Sure, you hurt your parents, but they must have forgiven you. You can never undo the past. Why not live in the present and turn your mind away from the past?

This is the Christian viewpoint. "Sufficient unto the day is the evil thereof."

My Late Wife

QUESTION: *I have been married for twenty years and have two teen-age children. There is one problem that worries the very devil out of me. My wife is eternally late. I have tried setting the clock ahead, calling her names, trying to reason with her, and nothing seems to do any good. Do you have any suggestions? I am afraid my children are going to be like my wife.*

ANSWER: I know exactly what you are talking about. I have been married twenty-five years, and my wife has the same problem; but I love her just the same.

Believe me, you are fighting a losing battle. I have told my wife that the reason the Bible speaks of a second resurrection is that she will not be able to get up on time for the first one. I, too, have called her "the late Mrs. Hudson,"—although your names may have been stronger.

The fact is, you have been married long enough to stop trying to reform your wife. I tried for the first twenty years, but finally woke up. Getting a wife or husband is like buying a Victrola record; you buy it for what you want on one side and you have to take what is on the other side.

Quit tantalizing your wife. She probably has a compulsion to be late. And fussing won't change her. As for the children, they need to respect both of you with your individual differences, without playing one against the other.

There are other ways to get the devil out of you besides worrying. Try praying for patience. You probably have some disgusting habits yourself, such as the compulsion to be on time. Some people are plain "nuts" on the subject of punctuality.

Wife Loves Another Man

QUESTION: *I married when I was eighteen and am now nineteen. My husband is overseas, and I feel that I am in love with another man. My husband says he loves me, but I do not love him. Should we go on through life and both be miserable, or should I write a "Dear John" letter and get it over with? What does God expect of me under the circumstances?*

ANSWER: How do you know that you do not love your husband? Or that you love the other man? Perhaps you are simply lonely, and this other man came along at the wrong time.

No, I wouldn't write a "Dear John" letter. The least you can do honorably is to wait until you see your husband to tell him. You might even learn to love him. You must have had some reason for marrying him in the first place. Consider this.

It is easy for a person to love someone until she lives under the same roof with him for a few months. Then you either mature in your love or you begin to hate him because of his limitations. This "other man" might not be so glamorous after you wash his dirty socks for about six months.

The Bible teaches that marriage is for life. Without this, there is little security in the husband-wife relationship. I have an idea that God would want you to row a while, and a little harder, before you give up the ship.

Loveless Marriage

QUESTION: *I have been married to a fine man for several years, and we have three children. I married real young and did not know what love was. Now I am in love with another man. I do not believe in divorce. Even if we were to get a divorce, the children would go with him, for he is such a fine, affectionate man.*

Should I continue to live with a man whom I do not love?

ANSWER: I doubt if you know yet what love is. It involves unselfishness and loyalty and trying to make the other person happy. Would you do this to your husband and children if you loved them? No amount of explaining would ever satisfy your children's questions.

You need to find out what is wrong with your marriage. Are you jealous of your children? Do you feel that your husband does not love you? Are you capable of giving and receiving love? Something is wrong, something basic. And it is likely right inside you.

You can do one of two things. First, if you could find a competent marriage counselor, perhaps you could discover the real cause of your discontent. It is emotional or spiritual. People just do not live together long enough to have three children without loving, if they are reasonably mature. If you are not mature, you wouldn't be mature with a second husband for long.

The other solution, a moral and religious one, will be difficult but worth the effort. Stop this flirtation and give to your husband and children what is rightfully theirs, your love. God can be of real help to you here. I have seen some great Christians come out of romantic love problems.

I'm not unsympathetic with you, but I just do not believe that your love for this new man is genuine. I have seen too many similar cases.

Husband's Parents

QUESTION: *Since we married, the only time I have heard my husband pray was when he became upset or frustrated about something. He would run to the bathroom and pound the walls, crying out God's name in a persecuted, rebellious attitude.*

Once I tried to explain my husband's attitude to his parents. They replied, "Our son was the shy, quiet type, who helped his mother around the house and never answered back. If you can't get along peaceably with him, that's too bad. We have nothing to say of his conduct now."

Is that the correct attitude?

ANSWER: Really, now, what did you expect your husband's parents to say? Why did you go to them in the first place? You didn't expect them to straighten him out, did you?

You had better be thankful that your husband prays instead of cursing or drinking. At least, he has a vague idea that God is his source of help, even if only in time of trouble.

Your husband has a problem. It may be you. But whatever it is, you cannot solve it except as you create the environment for growth. I suspect that the best thing you can do is to learn to accept your husband as he is, pray for him, set a good example, and try to make life as bearable as possible for him.

Dogs Ahead of Family

QUESTION: *Do you think it is a sin for a man to put dogs, women, and whisky ahead of his family?*

My husband is a fox hunter and spends so much on his dogs that the children and I do not have clothes good enough to go to church.

ANSWER: You remind me of the woman who said that, though she did not believe in reincarnation, if she should ever come back to this earth she would like to be her husband's hound dog. She gave three reasons: If she should get up in the night, he would immediately arise to see what was the matter. Second, if she got the least bit sick, he would take her to the doctor. Finally, she would be allowed to sit on the front seat of the car.

If your husband puts these things first, you have a poor marriage. Of course it is a sin. But you are making a mistake, too, unless your clothes are much worse than those of most people who give this as an excuse for staying away from church. Do you have clothes good enough to go to other places? Then they are good enough to go to church.

Your best bet is to lead that husband to Christ. In the meantime, set him a good example of Christian living. Prayer and Christian love can do wonders for a home.

No Longer in Love

QUESTION: *My husband and I are in our early fifties and have a twenty-year-old daughter in college. A few months ago my husband told me very calmly that he no longer is in love with me and, to be fair to me, he would like his freedom. To help him financially I have to work outside the home. He won't take me anywhere any more—not even to church.*

What has happened to him, and what would you suggest that I do?

ANSWER: My first impulse is to tell you to see a lawyer and have him throw the book at this man. But on second thought, there may be a better way.

Some men in their fifties go over fool's hill just like teen-age boys. They are declining in many ways and wish to have their last fling at youth. It is pathetic, but comes as a result of arrested emotional development.

Is your marriage really that bad? If he hates you strongly enough, nothing can be done. But my guess is that, if your husband has any moral principles, he will get over this feeling and work out a reasonable adjustment to you. Be patient. Only God knows what he is going through.

If I were you, I would not give him a divorce except as a last resort. Be a good, sensible, kind, human wife and see if you cannot make the home so pleasant that he couldn't find a better one if he tried.

Called But Cranky

QUESTION: *Our home is about to be broken up. My husband says he is called to preach and he preaches occasionally when he is invited by some church. But I am about to lose my mind. He fusses, criticizes the children, expects them to act like grownups, and keeps everybody in an uproar. We are all afraid of him; it is like being in prison.*

What can we do?

ANSWER: If your husband is as bad as you say, he is in bad shape. In fact, he is spiritually sick. It is certainly a dreary picture. You failed to tell me how this would look from his side. Suppose you try sitting down and writing for him a letter about how he sees you and the children. Make it about ten pages long. Tell all of your bad qualities, as he has no doubt spoken of them to you many times. Then burn the letter. No one will be interested in reading such hate.

Look at it this way. Your husband is either sick or mean. If he is sick, you should not hate him or blame him for it. If he is deliberately mean, only God can change him.

There is no use in taking a defeatist attitude toward your situation. You can divorce this man, nag him about changing his behavior, turn the children against him, or talk about him to the neighbors and relatives.

Or you may stay sane and try to help the children to take the best possible approach to a very bad situation. Christ would have us do the best we can under the worst conditions.

Maybe he is called. Maybe not. That is between him and God. Don't meddle with it.

You might remember the advice of the late Julius Rosenwald, president of Sears Roebuck and Company: "When you have a lemon, make lemonade."

Husband Wants Divorce

QUESTION: *My husband and I have lived together for twenty-one years. We have six children; the three youngest ones are in their teens, when they really need a daddy, but my husband wants a divorce. He has broken up another man's home and says that he does not love me any more.*

I don't believe in divorce because the Bible is against it, but what am I to do? I cry and pray and beg him to give up this woman, but it does no good.

ANSWER: What can you do? If you have any kind of justice in the courts of law in your part of the world, the judge will make this creature that calls himself a "man" provide for you and your children. It is a little late after twenty-one years for your husband to decide that he doesn't love you. I would sue him for everything he has and everything he can make for the rest of his life. That last sentence is an exaggeration, of course. Don't get revenge, even by law. It never pays. But you have a right to economic support after bearing a man six children.

Perhaps there are reasons for this man's leaving you. That is worth thinking about. Even middle-aged women can remain attractive, interesting, and affectionate, if they have the will to do so. How much do you weigh? Do you watch complexion and disposition? Are you a good cook and a good housekeeper? Crying and begging are poor techniques for winning back a wayward husband. Why don't you try being such a delightful wife that only a fool would leave you?

Home Breaking Up

QUESTION: *Our married life has consisted of many sorrows and struggles. My husband has always been self-willed and stubborn. His treatment of me has been beyond description. I am never considered a partner in business affairs, except to blame me when things go wrong.*

To top it all off, he has been "stepping out" on me for quite some time. He has even chosen another color, who is, or was, available for the general public. Right now (for about two months) she has been in jail, so that has temporarily closed the affair. But he has not changed and may find another.

My home is at the breaking point. I have been sick a lot, but that does not excuse him. We are past middle age and have grandchildren. What can I do?

ANSWER: I can understand how desperate and humiliated you are. Your greatest problem is within your own heart. If you can, by prayer and forgiveness, overcome your "hurt" you will be a rare woman. Perhaps only time and the grace of God can heal this wound, and even change your husband, but I doubt that leaving your husband is the solution. Men have been known to come to their senses and to straighten out.

What your husband needs is help. Perhaps he can be persuaded to turn to his pastor or the family doctor for counsel. However, this is not too likely.

Try to handle your hostility on your knees. The chances

are that your husband has "stepped out" on you as an act of hostility toward you. It is not just sex drive that makes men or women unfaithful. But you cannot overcome hate by expressing hate. Try love. Some of these days he will try to show some understanding and kindness to you. When he does, be prepared to meet him more than halfway.

Prodigal Husband

QUESTION: *My husband has left me five times. His folks, to whom he returns, tell him how foolish he is to live with one woman instead of getting out and having fun. Now, after months of separation, he comes back again and says he has never been happy and wants to come home. He professes to be a Christian, but seems unstable. What should I do?*

ANSWER: What makes you think he is any different now from the other times? Some women have an unconscious need for punishment, and you seem to be one of them.

If I were you, I would find a minister or a marriage counselor, and both of you sit down with him (or her) and examine this whole picture.

My guess, on such slight knowledge as your letter gives, is that your husband is not sure he is a man, therefore has to assure himself by chasing other women. There is probably not an assured male in his family. You will not save him by taking him back. Unless he changes by facing his own character defects in the sight of God, it sounds to me as if taking him back would be the last thing I would do.

Keep praying; there may be hope.

Ex-Wife Threatens

QUESTION: *Four years ago I married a man who had been married before. He was thirty-two, and I was seventeen. His former wife and their little girl live close by and she writes both of us letters saying how much she loves him and begs me to free him. Now she threatens to move in with us if he does not start helping her more. We pay all the child's doctor's bills now and help all we can. But we are buying a little home and don't have much money. My husband just laughs at these threats, and then we fuss. What can I do? We work in the church regularly and try to live like Christians.*

ANSWER: It sounds to me as if you married a mistake instead of a man. Any man ought to have sense enough to know that such letters are a great threat to your security. Laughing at your concern is a pretty low blow.

It seems to me that you have only two possibilities. Sit tight and pray that she may not carry out this threat. Incidentally, if she tries to move in, a few handfuls of hair pulled out the minute she darkens your door might help to answer your prayers.

I'm not recommending this, but if your husband is not man enough to protect you, it will be necessary for you to defend yourself. The other possibility is to get a divorce. I cannot recommend that, either.

Maybe God has a better way. Go slow and pray. He will show you.

A "Mean Woman"

QUESTION: *I have a very sad problem. I have been married for thirty-three years and have two boys and a grown daughter. My husband has left me and the children for a mean woman who lives down the road from us. I am not a Christian but am having a lot of sorrow. What can I do?*

ANSWER: The first thing to do is to turn to Christ as your Savior. He will help you bear your sorrow. I have seen troubles such as yours cause people to be saved and give the church the place in their lives that it deserves. This may make a Christian out of you. Talk this over with a pastor in your community.

Why has this man left you? Have you nagged him? Have you grown old in spirit? What about your looks, your disposition, your love life with your husband? The first thing to do with any such problem is to understand its cause.

It seems to me that there are only two things that you can do. Divorce him, or wait for him to come to his senses and return. I would recommend the latter. Of course this woman is mean. Breaking up homes and breaking hearts is a low-down trick. Your husband and this woman do not have the moral right to do this to you and your (and his) children.

But you may win your husband back with the help of God and God's people. Give your husband something better than he left. Change. Or better still, let God change you. This problem is too big for you alone.

Mad Husband

QUESTION: *We are a family of five, my husband, my two daughters, my son, and I. All of us are members of the church and work in the church. To everyone outside our home my husband is nice. But at home he is awful. He curses, nags, calls me filthy names. Now the children are taking up the habit.*

We have been married eighteen years and he says that he is trying to run me off, that he is tired of supporting me. What can I do? Should I divorce him? Several times he has rededicated his life but he has not changed.

ANSWER: No, I would not divorce him. Not unless the situation becomes entirely unbearable.

You and your husband ought to sit down with some pastor or marriage counselor and see why he is so hostile toward you. A part of the trouble may be your fault. Do you try to dominate him? Do you make him feel guilty? Do you threaten his manhood? This man is suffering and needs help from some outsider who will help him to work through his hostility.

You would be surprised at what goes on behind the closed doors of some so-called Christian homes. But it is wrong. If a man cannot be Christian at home, he lacks something that a Christian ought to have.

However, I had rather have a husband who expresses his hostility through words than one who expresses it through drink, or immorality, or through coldness. At least, he is honest. He really hates you. Perhaps he is like the man who bragged that he had an even temper; he stayed mad all of the time.

Love this man. Pray for him, as Christ said. Do not return his hate. You may win.

Grouchy Husband

QUESTION: *My husband and I have been married for more than thirty years. For almost four years now we have been in the house together twenty-four hours a day. During this time he has developed a terrible disposition, cross, grouchy, snappy, and pouty, never in a good humor. His attitude toward me is as if he hated me. He does not want me to go any place and criticizes me for talking across the back-yard fence to neighbors, calls my friends hypocrites.*

The hardest thing I've ever tried to do is to pray for him. It is difficult to love and appreciate him as I used to do. The doctor advises me to leave him.

ANSWER: Your doctor may be right, but I doubt it. You know more about your husband than any outsider. If you have lived with him thirty years, my judgment is that you may gain the inner resources to stick it out to the end. Of course your husband hates you. Don't you hate him? If not, why can you not pray for him?

My dear lady, human ill will is deep in the human heart. The closer people are thrown together, the more hostility comes out. This does not mean that you two do not love each other. Of course you do. But it means that somehow each of you is bringing out the worst in the other. This is very destructive and very anxiety-creating.

I think your husband is sick. If you will realize this and

deal with it as an illness, you will be more charitable and more realistic. Grouchiness is a childhood pattern which has become chronic in his case. Isn't there some kind of recreation that you two could participate in? Can you find some way that will frustrate him less? If not, and if he will not get scientific help, you should live with him if you can, or leave him if you must. Only God knows, but He cares.

Preacher's Wife

QUESTION: *I have been married to a preacher for thirteen years and have three children by him. But I do not love him. He knows that as well as I do. I am a Christian. I would like to be a nurse and have worked in three hospitals. I definitely do not like to keep house, but what am I to do? Should I continue living with my husband or should I leave him and become a nurse?*

ANSWER: We need Christian nurses, and I think that it is a wonderful profession. Also, I hate to see people live together in a loveless marriage. Perhaps with some help your marriage could be improved. If you are mature enough, you might learn to love him. I'm sure that he needs your love.

But it seems to me that you have too much involved to give up the ship. Your children deserve the security of at least not being saddled with the stigma of a broken home. Besides, what of your marriage vows? "For better or for worse" means something.

Quit debating leaving your husband. You can never build a sound marriage on uncertainty and indecision. If you love nursing more than your husband and children, there is something wrong with you. Try to get that something straightened out. You can find someone who can help you. Give yourself to your home, to your husband and children. Then what you give to nursing will be worth more. In any case, Christ will help you to take a creative approach to your very difficult problem.

Coaxing a Husband

QUESTION: *I am a person who likes to go to church, and try very hard to live a Christian life.*

My problem is this: When Sunday comes, my husband always finds some kind of excuse to keep from going. I don't want to press him too far. What must I do about it?

ANSWER: You have a sensible attitude. Don't press him too far. Men don't like to be dominated by women. It makes us feel that we are not real men. And the more we doubt our masculinity, the more we have to throw our weight around. No one method will work on all men, but every smart woman learns how to manage us. The following methods will usually succeed:

First, be very good and understanding to your husband. Never ridicule him nor make him feel inferior. Brag about him, feed him, love him, and ask his opinion.

Second, try to see why your husband does not like to go to church. If his reason is such that reasonable persuasion, prayer, and love cannot overcome it, give up. That is, accept the fact that if he changes, he and God must effect the change. Too many married people are trying to change each other.

Finally, love your husband as he is. Set him such an example of Christian living that when you die, he will want to spend eternity with you.

Unloved Husband

QUESTION: *Must a wife feel responsible for a husband's actions, like a mother? My husband tries to give the impression that everybody has failed him, even the Lord. He cries, cusses, and yells like a young child if anyone goes against him. I am much stronger than he is spiritually, and this infuriates him. It is hard for me not to be contemptuous of his childishness at times, but how can I help it?*

ANSWER: It is not uncommon to find a man who feels unloved, but it is rare that one comes as near admitting it as your husband does. No, I would not feel responsible for him, but I would try to understand that he is suffering and may continue to do so.

It sounds to me as if you have lost respect for your husband. Is that the correct approach? If he is suffering from a feeling of not being loved, he is suffering. That is all there is to it. I know that his demands are unreasonable at times and that it seems childish to you, but does he know any better way to meet this problem?

You might try confronting him (in an uncritical way) with the fact that God is trying to love him, and that you are, but that none of it seems to get through to him. Love requires a certain amount of faith. Perhaps you can help him to see that the trouble is inside him, and that you are not objective enough to deal with it. Be fair. Be frank.

If you cannot get your husband to talk his problem over with some trained counselor, there are only two possible alternatives: Either make the best of a bad situation and not be too angry about it; or get him active in the church, under

the sound of good teaching and preaching, and trust God to
change him.

Divorce May Be Criminal

QUESTION: *After a dozen years of marriage, my husband
wants a divorce. We are Christians, but he says that he no
longer loves me. My inclination is to refuse because of the
heartbreak to our two darling children, but my grief is so
great that occasionally they get a glimpse or suspicion of unhappiness. I love my husband, but would give him up if it
is best for the children. My husband says that he only feels
coldness, indifference (as well as respect) for me. What
would you advise?*

ANSWER: A marriage without love is very hard to bear.
Only the strongest can bear it. Sometimes such marriages
must be dissolved, even against our best wishes, but I do not
believe that a man and a woman live together twelve years
and bear two children without there being love. My guess is
that your husband loved you originally and can learn to love
you, in a more mature way, again.

I would like to ask your husband some important questions. When did he find out that he did not love you? What
had you done to kill his love? And what had he done that
might throw some light on his feelings? Is he willing to look
into his own emotional problems to work this out?

My experience is that many such problems can be solved
if the proper kind of counseling help is accepted. Is there no
family counseling center close to your home? It is downright
criminal and foolish to get a divorce under your circumstances, unless every means is used to analyze the situation

first. If your community does not have a trained counselor, turn to your pastor. Most modern pastors have some skill in these matters.

Unhappy Woman

QUESTION: *I've been married twice in the last ten years. Each marriage lasted only one year. Both of my husbands were Baptists, and I am a Methodist. They always went with me to my church, but I wouldn't go with them.*

My form of religion says that I can do as I please. I ran around on both husbands, and they caught me. The last one hasn't divorced me yet, but we have been separated for three years. I married him for his money.

I am not happy. What can I do?

ANSWER: Your most hopeful remark was, "I am not happy." How could you be? The question is, what are you willing to do about it? Do you want to change, or do you expect the world to change to your way of living?

First of all, the Methodist church does not teach that you can do as you please. I seriously doubt that you have ever been converted, and I think that if you are unhappy enough, there is hope for you to come to know Christ. You need to ask God to forgive you for using people for your selfish purposes. Nothing short of deep humility and thorough repentance to God will solve your problem.

Your "acting up" is a sign of a very childish attitude. You are empty inside, and nothing short of being filled with the Holy Spirit will ever satisfy.

The next time you marry—and there will likely be another —try to find a man who is not a weakling, one that you cannot wrap around your finger. You need some controls, both within and without.

The trouble with you is you. But there is hope, if you are dissatisfied with yourself.

Jealous Wife

QUESTION: *I am so very jealous of my husband, almost insanely jealous, that I know it is hurting our marriage. I don't know what to do. I don't want to be jealous, but I can't seem to help myself. It's almost like a sickness.*

ANSWER: It is a sickness, a disease of the soul. If you really cannot stop this, you must find someone to talk it over with who can help you to overcome it. A well-trained marriage counselor or psychiatrist or minister might be able to help you.

My guess is that you are a very dependent and possessive person. Because you have never become a true self, you try to live by becoming attached (hopelessly) to someone else. This is a very pathetic state, and you need to do something about it before it becomes chronic.

Your husband is an individual. If he is preferring someone else to you, if he is stepping out on you, this certainly will not be prevented by your clinging more closely to him. Marriages often go on the rocks because they were not good marriages in the first place.

Try to become more mature, yourself. God made you with enough good qualities for you to get along. Respect yourself. Learn to accept the limitations of life. Jealousy is an open confession that you do not value yourself.

Prayer and giving your life to the service of Christ would help too.

Wife Confesses

QUESTION: *My husband is in the armed forces. Once, while he was away from home, I fell into sin and went out with another man. Later I confessed this to him. He slapped me and then said he was sorry and that he would forgive me if I would forgive him. Later I became depressed and have been treated by a psychiatrist. But I still feel depressed and anxious. Do you suppose God and my husband can ever forgive me?*

ANSWER: You have a very complicated situation. Your husband cannot be expected to forget this overnight. He has been deeply hurt and needs help in managing his hostility. Perhaps he will need to see a counselor himself. Otherwise he may punish you without intending to.

Your problem is deeper. You need help from some Christian counselor who understands the human conscience. God will forgive you if you trust Him; so will your husband if he is a true Christian. But you must accept yourself as a sinner and learn to live orderly under God and with man. What good does self-punishment do? Does it make you a better person?

Quit punishing yourself. Live in the present. This is God's will for you.

Don't Run Away

QUESTION: *I'm thirty-four years of age, married for my second time, and I'm not in love with my second wife. I have been thinking of entering the Air Force and making a career of it. My wife doesn't want to go along. Would it be right for me to go? I have no future here and I am miserable. Do you think I could live a Christian life in the Air Force, where so many people are not Christians?*

ANSWER: I am not aware that the percentage of non-Christians is greater in the Air Force than elsewhere. Living the Christian life is not a matter of whom you are with, but how you stay in the will of God. You must accept God's guidance. He still makes His will known to people.

Yours is the old story. If you cannot love one woman, the next one will be little different. You say that you are not "in love" with your wife. The real question is, do you love her as a person? Can you give of yourself to her and receive from her?

You will not likely solve any problem by running away. You will still be miserable. If I were you, I would find some marriage counselor who could help you to see what is wrong with your present marriage and with you, and then try to change the things that are wrong. God will help you.

Should Husband Apologize?

QUESTION: *After twenty years of married life, only one thing still puzzles me.*

Ten years ago my husband became attracted to, and went out with, a woman a few times. When I knew it and mentioned it, he stopped at once, and definitely. He would never say that he was sorry for hurting me. Our only child (who doesn't know this) will marry soon. Should I mention this to my husband or go on, confused?

ANSWER: Why do you want your husband to say that he is sorry? Are you trying to punish him? Has not the fact that he has behaved himself for ten years proved anything to you?

I think you would be very unwise to bring this up after ten years. It seems to me that you are not dealing with your real problem. Either you do not feel secure in your husband's love, or you are trying to get revenge. Of course he is sorry. He made a fool of himself. He is probably so ashamed of himself that he never wants to think of it again.

You should accept your husband as a human being, a sinner, and help him to bear his sins, as Christ taught us. Even God does not ask us to say that we are sorry. Anyone can say that. He asks us to repent, to get a change of mind and heart.

If you will deal with your own childishness about this, and love your husband freely, you will probably never have this problem with your husband again.

Prodigal Husband Returns

QUESTION: *I was reared in a Christian home, but my husband was not. After he and I were married, he joined the church and was genuinely saved, I believe. His folks would not speak to me or come about our home.*

Finally his brother returned from service, and persuaded my husband to meet him in taverns. This proved too great a temptation, and soon he was convinced that one woman was not enough. He went from bad to worse.

Again and again he came back to me and tried to rededicate his life. Our four girls and two boys were devoted to him. But, finally, a year and a half ago I got a divorce. Now he comes back and says that he was never happy, that he wants to come back to me and to the Lord. What must I do?

ANSWER: Read the Book of Hosea and the prodigal-son story. But do not jump to conclusions.

Your children ought to have some sound opinions, and I believe they ought to have some say in the matter. But, no doubt, you are the one who has suffered most. Do you really think your former husband has changed? Or is he one of those persons with mood swings, and right now he is on the upswing?

Women are incurable optimists. This condition of your husband requires realism—looking at the facts.

Then you have to decide whether you are spiritually capable of forgiving. Some people aren't. If you are one of these, don't take him back until God gives you the grace to do it right.

Should a Wife Forgive?

QUESTION: *My husband recently told me he had lived a dog's life with another woman and that he had treated me like a dog for her.*

He asked me to forgive him and not to leave him. He said he was sorry that he did me that way for her. Will God forgive him? And should I forget it?

ANSWER: It sounds to me as if you have misunderstood what forgiveness means. It is not merely the cancellation of sin. God does not say, "Of course, I know you didn't mean any harm, so I will forget the whole matter." This is not what the Bible means by forgiveness.

Forgiveness means the restoration of a sound, working relationship. It means communion and fellowship.

Now if your husband will come back to God as a subject and allow God to use him, I know He will forgive.

Likewise, if your husband will treat you as a woman, instead of a dog, you can afford to forget the whole matter. But if he is asking you to forget about his past injuries to you and does not intend to change, that is another matter. Forgiveness means that you two renew fellowship on a mature love basis and that the past in no way enters into this new relationship.

So far as forgetting is concerned, only God can "remember our sins against us no more."

Is Husband to Boss Wife?

QUESTION: *My husband and I don't agree on what we should give to the Lord. He just won't give the tenth and won't give very much at all. We own our home and have a very good income. The Bible says that the man is head of the house; in other words, that he is supposed to be the boss. What am I to do?*

ANSWER: You cannot solve your personal, spiritual problem until you get straight on what the Bible teaches.

Where in the Bible does it tell wives to obey their husbands? It says, "Children, obey your parents in the Lord," and, "Servants, be obedient to them that are your masters," but nowhere does it tell wives to obey their husbands. This is false doctrine, propagated by a masculine society, and is untrue to the New Testament, which says that in Christ there is "neither male nor female."

It does tell woman to subordinate herself to her husband, to seek his leadership, to encourage him to be the head of the family under Christ. The pattern is Christ and the church. But does Christ boss the church? Does he lay down rules or edicts? Or does he lead the church in love? (Read Eph. 5:21–33 and Col. 3:18.)

Woman is supposed to subordinate herself to the man. She is made up that way. But when this becomes the husband's laying down the law about where the money is to be spent, man becomes ridiculous. Such matters ought to be decided in a democratic manner by discussion and good judgment.

It will take more than quoting Scripture ever to get woman back into slavery, thank God.

Does this answer your question?

Obedience of Wives Again

QUESTION: *You say in a recent column that "nowhere does it tell wives to obey their husbands." How could you write such a thing? This is to deny the very Bible itself and to preach false doctrine. What about Titus 2:5 and 1 Peter 3:1–6? Either I have the wrong version of the Bible or I cannot understand plain English.*

ANSWER: The Titus passage you mentioned is the only passage in the King James version of the Bible that uses the word "obey"—in speaking of the husband-wife relationship. And unfortunately this is a false translation, as every other translation shows. Look them up. Don't take my word for it.

The Williams translation says, "subordinate to their husbands." This is about as good as this can be translated. The Souter Greek lexicon says this verb means "I put in a lower rank, I rank under," a military term. The instruction to wives is the same as to all church members toward one another. "Submitting yourselves one to another in the fear of God" (Eph. 5:21). This is the same Greek word that tells wives to "subject themselves" to their husbands.

You see, the idea that wives are to obey husbands just as little children are to obey parents, or slaves their masters, is simply not a part of the New Testament. You ought to use a translation that was made since 1611. The new ones do not cost any more and are known by every living Bible scholar to be superior to the King James version.

Calls Church Unprintable Names

QUESTION: *My husband is a member of the Methodist church, but he always wants to go to my Baptist church with me. Each time he gets angry at me, he tells me that I can't park his car in front of my church any more. He calls my church unprintable names. Then when Sunday comes, he'll say that we are going to church, but I don't want to go because he calls my church such bad names. Sundays are blue and sad. Tell me what to do.*

ANSWER: Lady, don't be silly. Why should you stay away from church because you and your husband have had a fuss? Several other couples I know have passed around some unprintable names also. The church is not for illustrious Christians but for growing, struggling souls. And just because your husband calls the Baptist church unprintable names does not make it so.

I know of a college professor who told one of his students, a girl, to go to hell. She immediately went to the president. His brief reply was, "Well, I wouldn't do it."

Quit pitying yourself. Try to find out why your husband gets so angry at you so often. It may be your fault. If so, try to change, by God's help. But if you and your husband seem to have to hurt each other periodically, just take it in stride and learn how to get over it as quickly as possible. What you cannot change, you can live with. You might, at least, be glad that he will go to church with you.

There is a Christian approach to every problem—and being sad and blue is not a part of it.

✍ OTHER FAMILY PROBLEMS

Mother-in-Law Hate

QUESTION: *I cannot love my mother-in-law. We are Christians, and she is a good woman, but I feel guilty because I can't love her. It seems to be simply a personality clash. She seems to bring out everything bad in me. Outwardly we are nice to each other; we never "exchange words," but the way I feel makes me wonder if I am lacking in Christian grace. What can I do?*

ANSWER: Your problem probably goes back at least as far as Cain. Dear Adam never had this problem. And the devil has marred many an otherwise wholesome Christian by in-law hate.

You are really a bad woman, aren't you? You have evil thoughts, perhaps even murderous thoughts, about another human being, even a relative. My dear, nearly everyone you know has some secret problem like yours. Even good Christians. Quit trying to love your mother-in-law, in the usual sense. I think that you are trying to like her. Love her in the Christian sense. Accept her as she is. Don't be with her too much; maintain unbreakable good will toward her.

I'll tell you this: You will not overcome this feeling by simply reproaching yourself. Confess your weakness to God and do all of the nice things you can for your husband's mother. You may still feel the same, but you will be more intelligent in your approach to the problem.

Mother-in-Law Trouble

QUESTION: *Soon after we were married, my husband's mother came to visit us. She was giving me advice about how to manage my home, which I appreciated. Then she added, "Now I want you to study my ways and try the best you can to be like me, because I'm perfect!" I was so surprised that I knew not what to say.*

Can a person be perfect? What can I reply to my mother-in-law? She has been a Christian for many years and is a Sunday school teacher.

ANSWER: One thing I like about your mother-in-law, she said what she meant. That is about what most people mean when they try to reform or give advice to others.

Don't answer her. It will do no good. Perhaps you could learn some things from her—about how not to be. The best thing about her visit was her leaving, no doubt.

The studies show that the boy's mother breaks up more marriages than any other of the in-laws. Yours is a real problem. Even Christians are sometimes possessive and selfish, in spite of their religion.

No, you will never be perfect. (Read Matt. 19:17 and 1 John 1:8–10.) We are to aim at perfection (Matt. 5:48: "Be ye therefore perfect, even as your Father which is in heaven is perfect"); but all of my friends and relatives have missed the bull's-eye as yet. But they are still aiming.

Don't worry about your husband's mother. She is just trying to hold what she had for twenty years before you came on the scene. But you will win if you are smart.

Son-in-Law Trouble

QUESTION: *My daughter married a man who will not go to church. Recently she made a profession, but when the pastor went by to see her, he acted like a maniac. He cursed, and abused her, and talked terrible to me, and swore that she would never be baptized. She has four children now and says that she will leave him if necessary to join the church. Should I stop trying to get her to church? This is the only matrimonial difference they have had.*

ANSWER: Your last sentence must be an exaggeration. Pagan husbands just aren't that understanding about things other than religion. When a man blows as high as your son-in-law did over religion, there are a lot of other things that he is mad about.

I would stay out of this if I were you. Mothers-in-law ought to pray much and say little. This couple must be allowed to work this out their own way.

Try apologizing to the son-in-law and politely bow out of their religious squabble. Mothers-in-law just aren't the ones to convert sons-in-law, usually.

In-Law Trouble

QUESTION: *My mother-in-law keeps spoiling my wife, who is an only child. If she needs spoiling (which she definitely doesn't), I think it is my time now. My wife thinks I'm just jealous to want to deprive her mother of this pleasure, as she is all the mother has. But I would like to be the one to give my wife all these gifts and attention. Am I being selfish? What should I do?*

ANSWER: Have you tried looking yourself squarely in the mirror? Why are you so threatened by these "gifts and attention"? When a man marries a woman, he does not possess her body and soul. She cannot suddenly sever ties which developed for twenty years or so.

However, I know how you feel. It makes a man "second fiddle" to see the in-laws play such a prominent role in his wife's life. No one of us likes this. But you can hardly change your wife. She may change herself, if she is smart. But about the poorest thing a husband or wife ever tries is to reform their mate, and you certainly cannot change your mother-in-law. To her you are probably the villain who stole her choice toy.

I know that the Bible speaks of leaving father and mother. And this is very necessary. But as I know human nature, people leave their parents' household without leaving their hearts.

Try being frank with your wife. She probably has imagination enough to see that you are suffering over the situation. And my guess is that if she is a good Christian, she will gradually change. The Bible and the church can help here.

Real faith produces growth. In the meantime, enjoy the gifts your wife receives.

Illegitimate Parents

QUESTION: *My daughter, twenty-one years old, is going to have a baby out of wedlock. Our friends advise us to let her go to a home for unwed mothers and have the baby, then let the baby out for adoption. To me and to my daughter, this seems to be a sin. If we do this, we feel that we cannot go back to our church any more. Are we wrong in this feeling?*

ANSWER: You certainly are. The church should be a haven for sinners who are truly repentant, regardless of their sin. But the sinner must realize this as well as the saint. Everyone should go to church. The question of whether you should lead in the church depends on your influence and other factors.

You seem to feel that your daughter would be doing wrong to allow her baby to be adopted. This is a natural feeling. Your daughter has sinned, and there is a deep demand in most people that they be punished for their recognized sins. Also, it is natural for a mother to want to keep her own child.

But look at this from the child's standpoint. He (or she) will need a father. More than that, there is a certain label attached to a child born out of wedlock. He will go through life saddled with the stigma of illegitimacy. Actually his parents were the ones who were illegitimate in their behavior.

The Christian thing to do is to give this child a home where he and the neighbors will never know who his real parents are.

Sisters Quarrel

QUESTION: *My sister and I live together in a small apartment. We are both widows and above sixty years of age.*

My problem is this: We quarrel constantly and yet we seem to love each other. She objects to everything I do, and I know that it is not all her fault, for I am not easy to get along with. We are both Christians and go to church regularly. People would be surprised if they knew the truth. What should we do? I have thoughts of moving out, but that would be difficult.

ANSWER: No, I would not move out. Then you would either face loneliness or trouble with someone else. I think your biggest problem must be your own guilt feelings. When people feel hostile toward someone they almost invariably punish themselves. They feel mean. Or are depressed. Certainly they lose some of their self-respect. This is very disturbing, and the easiest thing to do is to run away.

Perhaps you and your sister are draining off some of your anger in these quarrels. They may not be all bad. And I will bet that you love each other much more deeply than you realize.

Read Ephesians 4:26 ("Be ye angry, and sin not: let not the sun go down upon your wrath"), and see if you cannot work out a better technique of "getting over" your troubles. Remember that either love or hate has to be cultivated.

Can't Stand Children

QUESTION: *My mother-in-law claims to live above sin, and tells her children that if she sins, she doesn't know it. Yet she says that she just can't stand children. She hates them.*

We have two very active boys, ages thirteen and ten, and they annoy her very much. But she believes in being the center of attraction, staying in our home about half the time. All of this makes me wonder if she knows the Lord at all, especially if she hates children.

ANSWER: Only the Lord knows for certain who His children are. Try not to judge. Of course your mother-in-law is wrong. The Bible says that "if we say we have no sin, we deceive ourselves, and the truth is not in us" (1 John 1:8). And this means exactly what it says.

On the other hand, there are some twisted people in religion who cannot stand to admit the truth about themselves. It seems to me that they need to join the human race—then apply for grace, like any other sinner.

If your mother-in-law hates children, there is a reason. Somehow they are a threat to her. Perhaps you do not even know why she feels so strongly about this. In that case, try to be understanding. Only God can change people. We can only create the environment for His redeeming love.

Hateful Sister

QUESTION: *My sister, who lives in another state, has accused me of some very bad things. I am living with my mother and caring for her the best I can. Recently a letter came from my sister in which she upbraided me for the way I treat Mother and even implied that my character is bad. This is far from the truth, as I have tried to live a good Christian life through the years, and my mother and I get along better than the average.*

My brother says that my sister is in that period when women sometimes get off the beam; but why should she take it out on me? Should I write my sister? As I feel now, I don't want to have anything to do with her.

ANSWER: When you want to help people in this world, you do not meet ill will with more ill will. Yes, I would write my sister the most understanding letter I could compose. Do not add to her load by making her feel guilty. Just explain your point of view the best you can. I suspect that your brother has the correct analysis of her condition.

Your real problem is hostility. Your sister has made you mad. Perhaps she has brought out some old feelings that you had toward her, at times, in childhood. Now what are you going to do about your own inner resentment?

Give yourself time and you will absorb your hostility. Think about her condition. Be honest with yourself about your own feelings, and every time you pray, ask the Lord to help you to be merciful toward your sister. That is the Christian way.

Frightened Children

QUESTION: *Three years ago I was told that I had only one year to live. I have a chronic kidney infection. My condition is critical, and I may die at any time, though I am still up and around.*

My problem is this: I have two small children, a boy four and a half and a girl a year younger. While I was in the hospital my relatives kept telling the children that if they were not good their mother would die. Now when I scold them they cry and say, "Don't die, Mother; we won't do it again." This breaks my heart, for I am afraid that when I do die they will feel that they are to blame. How can I relieve their minds of the horror that lurks there?

ANSWER: I cannot imagine your relatives doing such a thing to your children. But unfortunately adults often try to control children by fear. It is a great mistake. But you can likely overcome a part of the harm.

In the first place I would do everything possible to avoid creating guilt feelings in the two children. Punish them if you need to, but let them know that when the punishment is over, the matter is settled. Never shame them nor try to make them feel that they are terrible children. They are just children who need external controls to support them as they grow. You can be that control.

Then I would explain to them very frankly that there is no connection between your sickness and their conduct. They are old enough to understand. Tell them that the relatives were dead wrong and that they tried to scare them because they wanted them to behave. Put it in a child's language.

Help them to see that all children are naughty at times, but that they will outgrow it. Accept their childhood. You can do that and be firm at the same time.

Boy Who Steals

QUESTION: *My eleven-year-old son has been stealing things. My husband and I live on a farm and raise tobacco and milk cows. Our boy is a good worker, but he seems to get lonesome, and some of his boy friends tell him that he is doing too much work for his age. He seems to be discouraged and to feel sorry for himself. He has nice clothes.*

We all go to church but we are not good Christians. We do not have the blessing at the table nor talk about God's work and His Word. I'm afraid we have been too interested in making money. Our boy joined the church a year ago and seems to be interested. But what in the world are we going to do about his stealing?

ANSWER: You did not tell me what or how much your boy steals. This is significant. Why do you think he steals? To hurt his parents or to get something that he wants? Most children steal a little at some time or other. You will not solve your problem simply by making your boy feel guilty. He knows that he is wrong. On the other hand, he must stop it.

Put yourself in your boy's shoes. Take him into your confidence as a self-respecting, reliable human being. His behavior is understandable, and he will explain it to you if you will listen and not browbeat him. Give him a share in the farm work, something of his own to be proud of.

If this does not work, talk the whole problem over with

your pastor or your school principal. They will keep confidences if you ask them to. But most of all, treat your boy like a human being. Trust his growth processes. If he is really a Christian he will overcome this if he loves and trusts his parents.

Have Mercy on My Son

QUESTION: *My fourteen-year-old son is going through some kind of crisis, and I don't understand it. Nothing seems right with him any more. He criticizes me and his mother. He fights with his younger sister. He criticizes the church. He even talks as if he is losing his faith. Do all boys this age go through such a crazy period? And what am I to do?*

ANSWER: The Lord have mercy on you and all parents who have teen-agers who are trying to "bring up their parents." No, they do not all act that way, but most of them do. They blow hot and cold. They love and hate, act civilized and pagan. Your boy is trying to grow up. He is neither a child nor a man. As someone has said, "He is too old to sit on his mother's lap and too young to take a girl out; too old to cry and too young to cuss."

If I were you I would try not to get too excited about my boy. He needs some stable person to bounce against. Let him know that you believe in him and can trust his growth processes. Give him a little more rope all the time but don't be soft. Anything you do will seem wrong at the time, and you will often be scared to death. But don't try to break his will; it will ruin him.

Pray for him and set him a good example. Never deceive him under any circumstances. Really, most of the time, the only thing you can do is to "stand by him and stand out of his way," and hope for the best.

Homosexual Boy

QUESTION: *I am a nineteen-year-old boy with homosexual tendencies. There has never been an overt act, but the urge and the accompanying feelings of guilt reached such a high degree of intensity that last July I consulted a psychiatrist. Since then I have been undergoing psychotherapy without improvement, so far as I can tell, even though he was recommended by the Academy of Medicine. He is a Reform Jew and doesn't seem to understand my feelings about this being a sin as described in Rom. 1:26–27. Should I continue with this psychiatrist or seek help elsewhere?*

ANSWER: The real question here is not the religion of the psychotherapist, but whether he has the right attitude toward your own decisions. If he is a good therapist, he will leave you free to make up your own mind about right and wrong. Maybe you are trying to get him to think for you or to make decisions for you. This often happens.

Psychotherapy is a slow process, and your type of difficulty is sometimes hard to cure. But think what it will mean to you to go through life without having to be molested with these thoughts and feelings. There is real hope for you if you feel as guilty about this whole matter as you seem to. The most Christian thing you can do is to stay in therapy until you have achieved a reasonable degree of comfort and maturity. And I would not change doctors unless I had given this one a fair trial. The religious part of your difficulty may be worked out with some trained minister.

61

Domineering Father

QUESTION: *My father and brother and I are in business together. For the last three years we boys have had increasing difficulty with him. He is domineering, loud, and profane. I am a deacon in a Baptist church and my brother is a Christian and a church member.*

Here is our problem. Dad cusses, bawls out the employees, criticizes us and Mother (who helps in the office), and generally makes everybody miserable. My brother has stomach ulcers, and I am having a skin circulation problem which the doctor tells me is caused by my emotions. We have too much money invested together to pull out of the business. What can I do?

ANSWER: You have a particularly difficult problem. When a boy feels extremely hostile to his father, it is almost impossible to keep from punishing himself in some way. If he does not feel justified in expressing hostility, he is almost sure to "take it out" on someone else or end up with a depression.

Can you realize that your feelings of fear and anger (or resentment) at your father are perfectly natural? Even Christians still have normal emotions. Revise your concept of yourself. As a "sinner saved by grace," which your religion teaches, you will feel some extremely violent emotions. The Christian solution is to admit the emotions but resist the pattern of destruction. I'll bet that you are telling yourself that if you were the kind of Christian you ought to be, you would not feel so hostile toward your father. Be honest with yourself and handle your father as intelligently as you can.

Family Altar Problem

QUESTION: *We have tried to have a family altar at our house, but for some reason it doesn't seem to work. I have two little girls and I think it would be good for them to read the Scripture and pray regularly, as well as for us. But here is my problem: it always seems awkward and embarrassing. To me, especially, it just seems unnatural to suggest it. So what we have done is to have it a while and then give it up. What is wrong?*

ANSWER: Many people have had your experience. I suppose that is why so many Christians neglect family worship. Perhaps you feel guilty. Some Christians think that prayer and Bible reading are only for the near perfect. Therefore they give it up. They do not claim to be very saintly.

Look at it this way. It is extremely easy for the presence of God to gradually fade out of our lives. We forget Him. We neglect to think about Him.

If your family can talk this matter over and agree on a regular period of worship, you may help yourself. Try to be frank with them about it. Religion must always be voluntary.

Then, too, talk this over with God. He will lead you. He may even help you to be a little bolder about your religion. It will help to be honest, though a bit embarrassed.

Middle-Age Delinquency

QUESTION: *My husband is past fifty, and three of our children are in full-time Christian work. Also, we have grandchildren.*

Recently I had a telephone call from a man in a distant city, telling me that my husband and a woman there are going together. Both my husband and the woman admit that they have been out to dinner, on picnics, and at parties, as well as at her house, together. He insists that he wants to continue living with me but that he also wishes to continue the "affair" with the other woman. What am I to do? We have been married thirty years.

ANSWER: Some middle-aged men make fools of themselves. Sometimes it is due to the fact that they feel themselves losing their youth. It is the psychological equivalent to the experience some middle-aged women go through. It is a kind of adolescence in reverse. This does not mean that I am excusing his behavior. Only God can judge your husband. He must find the resources, within himself, and from God, to overcome this wild behavior.

It seems to me that you ought to try every means to win him back. Thirty years of marriage is a great deal to throw away. By confidence in him as a person, and by acceptance of whatever anxiety he is having (that causes this affair), you will come nearer solving your problem. It may take years. But prayer and patience will help much more than nagging or punishment.

↝ LOVE AND COURTSHIP

Eager Spinsters

QUESTION: *We are three schoolteachers between the ages of twenty-five and thirty-five. We would like suggestions as to how and where to meet eligible young men. We don't mean just any person, but ones who have Christian ideals. We read such advice as to go to church where such fine people are to be found. We are Christians and have gone to church all our lives. Most social life outside the church is undesirable for Christians. What are we to do?*

ANSWER: Yours is a very serious problem. Some very stupid people will laugh at your plight and trot out the old chestnut that "an old maid can be as happy as anybody—after she quits struggling." Not funny!

The facts are that we have more men than women in our country, especially in the big cities. And many men are just too immature to risk marrying. And you can bet your bottom dollar that you are a lot better off than some of the married women I know. Keep hopeful but not eager-beaver. Be prepared for marriage if it should come. Learn to accept men, imperfect as we are. I know a number of unmarried women who want to marry a god. Since the days of the ancient Greeks, there have not been many of them available.

In the meantime build a rich, creative life with as much closeness to people your own age as possible. Go places, do things. But keep in the center of God's will.

If I ever get time I want to start a Christian lonely-hearts club, for just such people as you three. It is badly needed.

No Good as Husband

QUESTION: *A man twenty-five years of age came to our little town on business. I dated him and fell in love with him before I found out that he has a wife and a little baby boy. He wants to marry me, but he drinks and runs in debt and has some other bad traits.*

What am I to do? I feel dependent on him and cannot break with him.

ANSWER: If you cannot break with him, something is wrong with you. You need help. It may be that you have an unconscious need to get hurt. Many people do. Sooner or later you will find yourself up a dead end street.

This man tells you that he is in love with you and feeds you the usual "sugar pie" line. He did that to his wife, also. He seems extremely sincere and is a good talker, but is just weak. Is that right?

I have described some of the qualities of what is called a "character disorder." These people rarely improve. The other characteristics are: failure to conform to the rules of society, lack of realism, inability to stay long in one place or on one job, and very superficial relations with friends.

Often they write hot checks, drink, are immoral, and use dope.

If you marry this young man you deserve the worst. And the worst will be much worse than you have imagined.

Turn to God and turn loose of this playboy.

Prospective Husband

QUESTION: *I am seventeen and engaged to a boy twenty-eight. We think we love each other, but some difficulties are in the way. He gets drunk but not around me and will not talk to me about it. He fails to show up for dates and will not give a reason, but just changes the subject. When we are out with other couples he acts as if he doesn't even see me. He gives me expensive gifts, and my parents like him. Will this marriage work out?*

ANSWER: Don't marry the guy. If he won't talk to you now, six months after the wedding you can't pry his lips open. The mistake you made is in having a second date with him when he stood you up once. People who are too immature to keep their word, or to at least talk about it, are too immature to get married.

A husband must be chosen on the basis of (1) whether he is comparatively mature, (2) whether he can love unselfishly, (3) whether he is the kind of person you like to be around, (4) whether he respects and loves you enough to want to make you happy, and perhaps as many more similar spiritual qualities. Gifts, a flashy personality, and even good economic rating do not necessarily make for a good marriage.

Uncertain Bridegroom

QUESTION: *I am thirty-three years of age and going with a girl who wants to get married. We have discussed plans for marriage, but somehow I seem uncertain. She is a fine Christian girl, and our backgrounds are similar. I have prayed about this and talked to my pastor but I still feel that I am not ready for marriage.*

What should I do now?

ANSWER: I think you need help in understanding your problem that cannot be given on paper. It sounds to me like an emotional blocking that could be analyzed by an expert counselor. You may be afraid of the marriage relationship. You may be in love with your mother (I mean nothing disgraceful). You may be afraid of women or have them on too high a pedestal. Or you may be unconsciously rejecting all women.

Marriage is too important to enter into with reservations. Yet you are old enough to get married, if you are ever to marry. This problem ought to be worked out before marriage, it seems to me. If you cannot find a marriage counselor, or psychologist, or psychiatrist, or trained pastor who will work this problem through with you, you will simply have to use your own judgment. But if you go to a counselor, do not expect to get to the bottom of your trouble in two or three interviews. It usually takes much longer.

Often people marry with some misgiving. If God leads you, do not be afraid. Marriage is a great institution. It deserves your best. Most marriage failures could be prevented. I admire your good sense in trying to lay a sound foundation.

Woman's College Girl

QUESTION: *I am a college freshman and will be twenty years old in June. In all my years of adolescent growth, no boy ever asked me for a date, and I never had a boy friend. I am a Christian and want very much to marry and have a Christian home some day.*

Under the circumstances, do you think that I did wrong in choosing a woman's college instead of a coeducational institution? Do you think I should change schools?

ANSWER: Not necessarily. Many women's colleges provide ample opportunities to meet boys. And the environment of some women's colleges is often very good for girls, even better than coeducational for some girls.

But your case worries me. There are girls who should not marry and who find God's will and a good social adjustment in "single bliss." Look, if you really want to get married you must learn how to date. Romantic love is good: it is often wonderful. But you cannot learn how to relate yourself well to men out of a book. Social skill comes from social experience.

The most wholesome thing about your letter is your wanting to marry and have a home. That is good and right.

If I were you, I would try to be around boys, even if I had to change schools. We men are not so bad, once you learn to overlook our faults. Take a real interest in us, flatter us a little, mother us slightly, and we will fall all over ourselves.

Prodigal Son

QUESTION: *Our teen-age son had everything it took to be a good boy and a child of God. A few months ago he started going with a bad girl. We have known the family for many years, and they do not try to live right. Now our boy tells us that he has done wrong, and a baby is to be born.*

ANSWER: I hardly know where you should start on this problem. But of one thing I am sure, this affair between your son and this girl is not the basis for a sound marriage.

Your son has some great moral and economic responsibility in this matter. Girls do not seduce boys. And vice versa usually. But your son should bear his share of the reproach for this mistake.

Usually such matters are handled by the girl's going away to some home for unmarried mothers and then, when the baby is born, giving it for adoption. This plan has many problems connected with it, but it is one of the ways that such matters are cared for.

Your son needs all of the help he can get. He needs your love. He also needs your guidance in becoming a man.

But Christ would help these young people to build their lives on a better foundation. The Pharisees—they are still with us—will wish to stone them. If you pray and act with courage, you will find the way of truth and justice.

He Loves Me?

QUESTION: *I am a twenty-four-year-old bookkeeper and have been going with a young man about my age, off and on for three years. I don't have a chance to see him very often because he lives two hundred miles away. I love him and have even told him so. And if I can't marry him, I'll never marry. He says he believes that he loves me, but that he isn't sure. He also says that when he marries, he will marry strictly for love. But he has always had a hard time making up his mind. Do you think I should continue to wait on him to make up his mind or drop him and start anew?*

ANSWER: Aren't you being a little rash in saying if you can't marry this man that you'll never marry? It sounds to me as though you are putting all your "egos" in one basket. Let's be practical. When you have dated other boys, have you given them any serious consideration? How do you know that this boy is the one God has in His plans for you?

Really, I see no reason why you should drop him, but most certainly, since he has been so undecided, I'd cultivate other boy friends—and even consider them as possible mates for marriage. Perhaps this will awaken him to the fact that "he who hesitates is lost." A little competition is healthy for all of us, and it might even help him to make up his mind.

Now for his indecision. Don't you think he has been undecided for a long enough period of time to have come to some conclusion about your relationship? As for his saying he will marry strictly for love, that is a little unrealistic. Love affects people in different ways. Sometimes it is an "inexpressible alloverishness." Again it is a solid, quiet comfort. When this man is ninety, he may still be debating the question.

Remember everything does *not* come to him who waits! A little fishing in other pools certainly will do no harm! You might find God's will elsewhere.

On Marrying Divorcees

QUESTION: *What would you do if a young lady—member of your church—should ask you to perform a wedding ceremony (for her and her fiancé of another denomination) when you know that her family is definitely opposed to their marriage? Her parents, three of her sisters, and one brother are also members of the bride's church. Does the pastor have the right to go against the wishes of his members?*

ANSWER: It all depends on whether the pastor is serving under God or under the people. I always thought that a minister of the Gospel was to take his orders from the Lord.

If a couple came to me to get married, and all of the relatives on one side were opposed to the union, I would try to find out why. There is no reason to object to a marriage just because both do not belong to the same church. Do the churches differ radically? Can the couple get together on their religious beliefs? Have they found the will of God in their proposed marriage? These are the main questions.

Personally, I do not have much respect for a preacher who lets individual church members tell him what to do.

But I have far less respect for church members who profess to believe in the New Testament and at the same time try to dominate other Christians in their effort to find the will of Christ. Freedom is basic in Christian love.

If I were you, I would defend my pastor's right to do what he believes to be God's will in performing marriage ceremonies. He is an officer of the state and a servant of God. His being my pastor does not give me the right to push him around. If you do not agree with him, talk to him and try to persuade him differently. Do it in brotherly love. New Testament Christians do not coerce and threaten; they persuade and speak the truth in love.

Dominating Mother

QUESTION: *My husband has been dead for over a year. Now I have found a man with whom I am in love and who loves my children. But my mother, a widow, says that it will be sacrilege for me to remarry this soon. She says, "How can you think of marrying with your husband hardly cold in the grave." What should I do?*

ANSWER: Grow up. How could a woman get old enough to have children and still let someone else make her decisions for her? I do not know what your mother is thinking about. Does she want you to get set in your ways and accustomed to loneliness before you remarry? She is just as wrong as she could be.

I know a case very much like yours. The mother threw quite a fit when her widowed daughter remarried. She tried every way known to dominate her daughter and her grandchildren. But the daughter went ahead and married. Today

73

the mother is happy with her son-in-law and has admitted that she was wrong.

Be patient with your mother. But be firm. You must find God's will for yourself. But if you please God you may be forced to displease your mother. Read Matt. 10:35-37: "I am come to set a man at variance against his father, and the daughter against her mother, and the daughter-in-law against her mother-in-law. And a man's foes shall be they of his own household. He that loveth father or mother more than me is not worthy of me."

Love by Mail

QUESTION: *I am a girl of twenty-eight. I am writing to a man thirty-two, whom I have never seen. He writes me nice letters and wants to come to see me. I am a Christian. Should I let him come to see me or not? Do you believe in this kind of courtship?*

ANSWER: If you have every reason to think that your thirty-two-year-old man is honorable, and if you can see him in a fairly protected environment, I see no objections. There is nothing inherently wrong in a letter-writing courtship. Make plain to this man that you are a Christian and do not deceive him in any way. This is the Christian principle involved, just plain honesty.

Your circumstances are a little odd. But I have known of people who found mates through lonely-hearts clubs. It is not easy for some girls to meet the right man, and every reasonable means needs to be used. I rather admire your spunk. However, there are many unprincipled men in the world. Don't stick your neck out too far. And don't build up too great hopes. Some marriages are worse than old-maid-dom.

Girl Friend Drinks

QUESTION: *I am eighteen years old and try to live a Christian life. I met a sixteen-year-old girl and am in love with her. At least I want to help her. But she drinks. My friends tell me to quit her unless she gives up this awful habit. She does not want to drink but goes to the wrong parties. Should I quit her? Or how can I help her to quit drinking?*

ANSWER: My dear boy, never marry a woman to reform her. Romantic love and changing people usually do not mix. In other words, if this girl were really in love with you, she would quit drinking of her own accord, if she could. I do not see your girl's picture very clearly. It would be necessary to get some idea of when she drinks, how much, and why.

Christ has done wonders for some young people whom I have known. And He could for your girl. But if you are to be a witness to this girl, you will have to become a great Christian yourself. A good Christian hardly ever tries to stop someone from doing something, like drinking. He sets them such a beautiful example that they are naturally attracted to his way of life. Try that.

Confessing Past Sins

QUESTION: *In World War II I dated a man, and when he was ordered overseas we had intimate relations. I have repented of this and believe God has forgiven me.*

Now I am going with a man who loves me. Should I tell him of my past sins?

ANSWER: Why would you want to tell him? Do you still feel guilty about your former sins? Do you want to test him to see if he will reject you? Or could it be that you wish to degrade him a little?

If you are the kind of person who lives in the past, you will not make a good wife, anyway. And if he is so childish that he tries to pick your memory pockets, he will make a poor husband. I know that love is normally frank and open, and that some husbands and wives feel the necessity of unearthing all their skeletons. It seems to me that frankness should apply to the present, not to case histories.

But if you ever intend to tell him, do it before you marry him. Men do not like to be surprised. It hurts our vanity.

No, I would not tell him. He might use it against you in a family quarrel, some day. It might worry him or hurt his pride. Some men just cannot stand such information.

If he really loves you, as one adult should another, it would not make much difference. But many men are not capable of such mature love. If you really love him, why saddle him with the memory of your past failures?

If God has forgiven you, forget it. He has.

Not in Love

QUESTION: *I am engaged to a boy and sometimes I feel that I am tied down by being engaged to him. I am not the settling-down type and I know that I am not ready for marriage.*

We have been going together for four years and he says that if I return the ring, he will never date me again. He told me that maybe I had better stop seeing him for about a month and date other boys and make up my mind about him.

I cannot give him up and I cannot marry him. I like him but don't want to marry him. What should I do?

ANSWER: If this boy were half the man he ought to be, he would drop you cold. You are probably the type of girl who wants to have her cake and eat it too. I doubt that you are capable of loving anyone but yourself.

No, I would not marry at present. You are not ready for marriage. And a wedding ring will not cure your difficulty.

Your trouble is some deep emotional blocking. You need to see someone who will help you to see why you are not capable of love. But whatever you do, don't marry until you work your problem through with someone. You are a bad risk for a happy marriage.

Quit the boy. Then perhaps your anxiety will mount until you turn to some person who can help you. But you have no moral right to keep stringing this boy along.

✑ RIGHT OR WRONG?

Can a Christian Be a Movie Actor?

QUESTION: *I am a boy of twenty and hope some day to be an actor in the movies or on television. I truly feel that this is my talent and I believe that God sent me for this purpose in life. My mother tells me that I should not think of things like being a movie star.*

I am a Christian and am wondering if I am sinning or being worldly-minded by dreaming of this.

ANSWER: I don't know much about movie or television stars, but they tell me that it is a pretty strenuous life and very hard on a person's religion and morals. You certainly cannot afford to sell your soul, compromise, in order to be successful. Unless you are a rather strong Christian, you had better think of something less taxing.

Personally, I should like to see more fine Christian young men in Hollywood. The one-wife and loyal-to-Christ type. I hear that they are needed. We certainly need some top actors and actresses in religious films.

I'm sure your mother means well, but she doesn't know some of the fine Christian artists that I could name. It's your life, boy. God gave it to you and He is the one to tell you what to do with it. When the last whistle blows, you will have to answer to Christ. If God were to lead my child to be a movie or television artist and she were to do so without violating her Christian ideals, I should be proud of her.

Teen-Age Problem

QUESTION: *Our daughter is thirteen and wants to go to fellowship meetings after church. They are in the homes of nice people. My husband says that she is too young to start going places like that. She is the only one who can't. He doesn't approve of even light-colored lipstick, hose, or slight heels on her dress shoes.*

Am I wrong in thinking it is normal for a child to want to feel that she is part of her crowd?

ANSWER: Your husband is dead wrong. There is nothing more wholesome than for a teen-ager to be with other teen-agers. And I cannot think of a better place than at a well-planned fellowship after church. And as for light-colored lipstick and slight heels, when on earth does he expect her to start these things? They need to be introduced gradually.

A girl at thirteen has some real problems. She needs her father's love and respect even more than her mother's. If your husband could only see it, he has the chance of a lifetime with this girl. She needs from him affection (real, physical affection), understanding, kindness, and admiration. If she gets suspicion, fussing, condemning, criticism, and unfairness, it will be hard for this girl to believe that other men are reasonable and understanding.

When girls have unkind fathers, they often grow up to

feel unloved and inadequate. This is often back of immorality on the part of women, and especially of later maladjustments in marriage. When girls are not trusted by their fathers, they have a hard time trusting others.

You have a delicate problem. Stick to your husband and your daughter both. Keep channels of communication open, if possible. But, most of all, help each other to see that the Christian faith sponsors reasonableness and good common sense.

Teen-Agers' Dress

QUESTION: *What do you think of our Christian teen-agers wearing shorts and T-shirts and halters on the streets or anywhere in mixed crowds? Please answer this before the summer season is past.*

ANSWER: You do not really think that what I or anyone else says will change customs, do you? Not this summer. I think that Christians ought to dress, speak, and act in such a way that those who see them will not question their morals. But, personally, I do not believe that there is any connection between morals and dress. I have just returned from Mexico, where a woman would be arrested for appearing on the streets in shorts and a halter, but I doubt if the morals of the Mexicans are any higher because of this.

Any sociologist knows that there are very strict (morally) cultures where very little or no clothes are worn.

On the other hand, Christian women in America, particularly in smaller communities, will not want to have people talking about them for changing fashions. "Let everyone be fully persuaded in his own mind," is the word of Scripture. And, "Destroy not him with thy meat for whom Christ died"—referring to meat offered to idols.

It seems to me that we ought to give teen-agers what guidance they will accept, but not make an issue of those things which will lead them to think that Christianity consists of clothes and customs. You can find bigger things to fuss about with teen-agers.

Sons of Ham

QUESTION: *I am wondering if you have ever seen the word "Negro" mentioned in the Bible. In Genesis 9:18–29 we have the story of the cursing of Ham. Were not his descendants to be servants of servants? I do not believe in the mixing of the races, especially the Negro and the white races.*

ANSWER: If you will consult any good Bible or secular encyclopedia, you will find there is no connection between the Negroid race and the Hamites. Or if you will read on in Chapter 10 of Genesis you will find that the descendants of Ham were Cush (Ethiopia), Mizraim (Egypt), Phut (?), and Canaan. None of these were Negroes, but Semites.

This idea that Ham's sons were Negroes is completely without foundation. It was never heard of by scholars until some people of this country made slaves of the Negroes and then tried to find some justification in the Bible.

The truth is, about twenty per cent of the Negroes of America are already of mixed blood. What shall we do about that? No, the Bible has absolutely nothing to say about mixing the races. Rather it plainly says that God "hath made of one blood all nations of men" (Acts 17:26).

This is the time for true Christians to search their own hearts and see if they are practicing the Golden Rule and the Parable of the Good Samaritan.

I wouldn't try to make "servants" out of the Egyptians, if I were you. We will do well not to try to keep some people down. No, the word "Negro" is not mentioned in the Bible. Neither is the yellow race, nor the red, nor for that matter the white race.

Divorced Couple

QUESTION: *How do my husband and I stand in the sight of our God? We both have been married before. My former husband divorced me, and my present husband's former wife divorced him.*

Please write in your column what is best for us. We go to church and are happy together. My husband is a Baptist and I am a Methodist. According to what I can find to read on marriage and divorce, we were not supposed to remarry.

ANSWER: Why did you and your husband not think of this before you married? Does your standing in the sight of God mean so little to you? And if you are "happy together," why do you not belong to the same church? These are important questions.

The question of how you stand with God depends upon whether you have accepted His Son as your Savior. We are not saved by works of the law but by grace through faith.

Now as to your remarriage, you must consider one question. What is God's will under the circumstances? It sounds to me as if you have made the teachings of Jesus into a kind of legalism, as the Pharisees did the Sabbath laws

(Mark 2:23–28). Jesus taught that marriage ought to be permanent. This is the Christian ideal. But to crucify individuals on a cross of legalism, New or Old Testament, smacks of Phariseeism. In other words, you two must decide what Christ would have you do in the light of his total teachings on love and mercy, not on one or two verses.

Man will probably look on the outward conduct, but God looks into the heart. Start where you are and live for Christ. This is my advice.

Chain Letters

QUESTION: *I am interested in knowing what is right about chain letters. I receive so many through the mail. You are supposed to read Matthew 17:20; if you don't, and don't write four letters sending them to your friends, you are breaking the chain and bad luck will follow you in three or four days. They tell of Mrs. So-and-So who got a pile of money for answering one, and so forth.*

What do you think of this?

ANSWER: Pure bunk! Downright superstition and ignorance! Sin and shame! That's what I think—that is printable.

Do people really fall for that stuff in the twentieth century? And in the midst of Bible-reading Christians? It is hard to believe.

If Mrs. So-and-So actually received a pile of money, it was dishonest. She got it at the price of stupidity. She preyed upon the childish fears of simple, unthinking people, and that was wrong.

If you are a Christian, for heaven's sake don't let anyone

frighten you with "bad luck" threats. All sorts of superstitions—refusing to walk under a ladder, knocking on wood, fear of black cats crossing the road, and all the rest—grow out of a sense of guilt. They are based on the feeling that God is against us. The Gospel of Jesus Christ will deliver us from these fears.

Throw chain letters in the fire. Pray for the conversion of their senders. And thank God for peace and love and faith.

The Christian Sabbath

QUESTION: *I am deeply concerned over the Christian Sabbath. A lady who works in a grocery store told me that she could tell when church is over, as the store filled with churchgoers. Am I radical? I had rather come home and eat little than be party to forcing people to work on Sunday. Am I old-fashioned?*

ANSWER: We are living in a day of majority-vote-morality. If the crowd does it, it must be right, is the viewpoint of millions. Sunday, the Lord's Day, in memory of Christ's resurrection, is no longer a holy day but a holiday. And while some Christians debate over whether we should keep Saturday or whether we should keep Sunday, the majority have completely lost their sense of the sacred. Holy ground is not on our list of modern real estate. And holy days are largely among the annals of superstition.

The only thing that bothers me about your letter is this: Are you worried about your own practices or those of your fellow churchgoers? If your own, then I would say that you are probably practicing exactly what Jesus would do if he lived today. But if you are critical of others, then I fear that you are judging, perhaps even playing God.

I wish the world were different. The only place I know to start making it different is by holding to my own inner convictions without disliking or criticizing those who differ from me. Believe me, this is not easy. And don't think I am not discussing the Sabbath question.

Picture Shows

QUESTION: *I am a girl eighteen years old and a Christian. I want to know if it is wrong to go to the picture show. Will you please explain to me the fifteenth verse of the second chapter of 1 John. It confuses me and I hardly know what it means.*

ANSWER: Are you trying to get me shot? Don't you know that there are people who will shed good, honest blood over this issue? No, I won't tell you. But I will tell you the principles by which you may wisely tell yourself. First, does it harm you or someone else to go to shows? Second, would it be right if all people went? Third, what effect does it have on your Christian testimony? Fourth, what does the Bible say?

This last I would have put first, except for your second question. 1 John 2:15 says, "Love not the world." John means by the "world" those things which destroy, harm, handicap, or deter a man in following Christ. The old puritans included in worldliness such things as laughter, reading novels, dancing on the village green, whistling on the Sabbath, making money, wearing beautiful clothes, and many others.

If I were you, I would think for myself on these matters. You have judgment. Pray. Be conscientious. Read the Bible. But, for heaven's sake, don't condemn picture shows and then sit by the hour and watch television.

Country Clubbers

QUESTION: *My wife and I are members of the country club in our town. We are members of the local Baptist church and have been for some years. My wife teaches a Sunday school class.*

At our club parties there is always drinking. To go to these parties and not drink simply does not work. We have run out of excuses for not going. Yet the contacts are good for my business. What shall we do? We cannot reconcile the two memberships.

ANSWER: Excuses? Does a man need excuses for standing on his own feet and thinking for himself? I do not like Limburger cheese and I'll be hanged before I will allow my friends to tell me what to do and what not to do. Surely, there are insecure people who will try to make you conform, but are you so weak that you have to obey in order to be liked? Such friends are not worth having.

Most church members who are trying to practice their Christianity follow one of two policies. Either they stay away from parties where drinks are served or they politely and firmly refuse to drink. You must decide for yourself what Christ would have you do. Read Romans 14:21 ("It is good neither to eat flesh, nor to drink wine, nor any thing whereby thy brother stumbleth, or is offended, or is made weak") and make up your mind. Social customs will never be changed by people who do not possess their own souls. Christians are supposed to create customs, not conform to them.

In our society, with from five to eight millions of alcoholics in it, it seems to me that your conscience ought to be troubled over this drinking problem. So-called "social drinking" is antisocial. You cannot run with the hounds and the hares both.

You are facing a very difficult personal decision, but your business is not worth your soul. Besides, the sensible people in your group will admire you for standing on your own feet. Do not, for the sake of Christ, allow social pressure to determine your morals.

Insane Husband

QUESTION: *A woman in my congregation has a husband who is a mental case. He has had electric shock treatments, been in and out of mental hospitals for years, and has had the brain operation called lobotomy. The psychiatrists diagnose him as catatonic schizophrenic.*

This good lady can hardly live with him. He is moody, stubborn, unreasonable, and more than once has walked off from their business with the checking account.

She wants me to tell her whether or not it will be wrong for her to get a divorce. And should she have her husband committed to a hospital? She wants to do what is right as a Christian.

ANSWER: A minister is often faced with problems like this one. Only the courageous and humble will feel safe in tackling them.

Does the lady need you to give her the answers? And if you do, will she not be equally in need of your "decisions" when later questions arise?

You can help her, however, to know that God is not a tyrant who crucifies human beings on a cross called Law. Divorce laws were made for man, not man for the divorce laws. She must, like all of the rest of us, pray and read God's Word, and then act according to her best light. Christ is the only one who has the answers.

Encourage this woman to take the psychiatrist's advice about hospital commitment. And furnish her an atmosphere where she can "talk out" her deep resentments toward her husband. This, it seems to me, is your best contribution. However, if she is so immature as to insist on your advice, do the best you can and give as little advice as possible. Listen and love. That is the best counseling under some circumstances.

Beating School Children

QUESTION: *Some boys in our school were whipped with a leather strap until the blood was cut out of their backs. They were whipped like animals. My boy was one of them. The accusation was "playing hooky," although our boy left school to drive another boy to a neighboring town to take a driver's test.*

Should we talk to the superintendent about this?

ANSWER: States ought to have laws against beating children. Where I live it is against the law for a teacher to strike a child, and it works. There are other ways of handling children besides corporal punishment.

However, your son was wrong in leaving school without permission. I would make it plain to him that groups have to operate by laws. Every game, including the game of life, must be played by the rules. And so far as possible, I would stand by the school authorities. Children have to learn discipline.

Talk to the superintendent, and the principal. Keep the lines of communication open. Be reasonable and assume that others are. Most of them are.

Teach your son to bear his mistreatment as best he can. Christ was mistreated but he did not get revenge. ("Who, when he was reviled, reviled not again; when he suffered, he threatened not; but committed himself to him that judgeth righteously—" 1 Pet. 2:23).

Capital Punishment

QUESTION: *The question of capital punishment has come up several times recently where I am pastor. I answered the question from the Old Testament Scriptures, but the people want to know if the New Testament Scriptures teach capital punishment. Would you answer this for me?*

ANSWER: Jesus assumed a normal penal code in Matthew 5:25–26 ("Agree with thine adversary quickly, whiles thou art in the way with him; lest at any time the adversary deliver thee to the judge, and the judge deliver thee to the officer, and thou be cast into prison"). And Paul referred to a law enforcement in Romans 13:1–4. But the question of capital punishment is not to be settled by a proof text. The real problem is the protection of society in an effective and just and Christian manner.

Human nature being what it is, I am not sure that society can be protected without the death penalty for some. Fear is a strong force in human life. Also, I am not sure but that death by law is the kindest thing that can come to some twisted personalities.

Too, one life taken may prevent the destruction of five others. It is not Christian to turn the other cheek to an abnormal person. It will not redeem him. At least, you do not have the right to turn your neighbor's cheek.

The best Christian approach to criminal persons is to work at preventing them where possible, and curing others when possible. But this is a large order. Until we find better means, and prove that the criminal can be changed, we ought to be one hundred per cent for deterring crime by capital punishment. The mentally twisted are always with us.

Segregation

QUESTION: *My pastor believes in segregation and he preaches that the South can work out their problems if the government will leave us alone. I believe firmly that segregation is a sin and that the Negro should be given equal privileges in every way. What should I do? Leave the church, talk to my pastor, or sit quietly and say nothing?*

ANSWER: This is one of the most delicate problems facing our country today. If we ever needed Christian tact and grace it is now.

Personally, I do not agree with your pastor, but I will defend to death a free pulpit. If a pastor is not free to preach what he believes is God's truth, he becomes merely the voice of the strongest pressure group. So the last thing on earth for you to do is to threaten your pastor with leaving the church or anything else.

Talk to your pastor. Do it in love. Plead with him to see your viewpoint, if you wish. Express your deep feelings to him. And then, regardless of his viewpoint, tell him how much you love him and that you will be loyal to him under all circumstances.

Of course, I would not leave the church. There are a few "floaters" who drift from one church to another every time trouble arises. "They toil not, neither do they spin." You ought to be big enough to live with people who disagree with you. But stick by your convictions also.

Christian Lawsuits

QUESTION: *I operate a small grocery store and am an active member of the church nearby. Some of my customers who are my fellow church members refuse to pay their bills. After we use every friendly method to collect these bills, is it wrong, according to the Bible, to use the law courts to force these people to pay me? We must collect in order to stay in business.*

ANSWER: The Christian teachings about social relations have often been made ridiculous by extreme literalists. We need to take the Bible seriously but not always literally. I judge that the passages that gave you the most trouble as you sued for a bill are Matt. 5:40 ("If any man will sue thee at the law, and take away thy coat, let him have thy cloke also.") And perhaps 1 Cor: 6:1–8. These are great passages, and mean something very important. There are no universal rules. The one from Jesus' lips is a vivid, startling, dramatic, half-humorous rebuke to revenge and retaliation. Our values must be such that we will not strike back under any circumstance.

The second one, from Paul, simply points up the fact that most troubles between Christians can be, and ought to be, settled by reason, persuasion, counsel, and out of court. Going to law before non-Christian judges hurts the Christian witness. But some church members won't pay their bills unless sued. If you do not collect them, you must charge them to customers like me (in the profit you make) or go out of business. Charging this food bill to other people is unfair. Besides, to allow people to dodge justice is contributing to vice and immaturity. Think that over and act accordingly.

◄§ WHAT DOES THE BIBLE SAY?

Baseball at Church

QUESTION: *I would like for you to tell me if I am wrong. I teach a class of juniors in Sunday school. I object to having the church grounds used for ball games and other kinds of recreation. I use Matt. 21:12–13; Mark 11:15–17; Luke 19:45–46; and John 2:14–16 for my beliefs. I get lots of questions from these juniors about this matter of recreation on the church grounds.*

ANSWER: All of the Scriptures you mention have to do with Jesus driving the money-changers out of the temple. To tell the truth, such Scriptures may be used to apply to such situations as yours. Of course, Jesus was objecting to two things: the dishonesty involved in their sales and their currency exchanges; and their using the worship place for business.

This latter is somewhat like your situation. You object to using the church lawn for recreation, but is the church lawn sacred too? And where are the children to play? In this day of commercialized amusements, the church ought to do more than condemn worldly recreation. It ought to provide something better. Playing is a part of life as well as praying. I had rather see these juniors play on the church lawn than have no place to play ball.

Besides, the church ought to be associated with joyful experiences of life as much as possible. Many churches are building recreation centers. This seems to be a very different case from that of money-changers and offering-sellers.

Ping-Pong at Church

QUESTION: *I would like your opinion of games in a church. Our young people play Ping-pong in the church basement, or did, until a group of older ladies in our church decided it was wrong. In order to avoid trouble, our pastor took the Ping-pong table out. Now our young people go to the Methodist and Presbyterian churches several week nights to play games there.*

ANSWER: I don't blame your young people. They know that there is nothing wrong with playing in the church basement. How could they respect a church which places more emphasis on the opinions of the eighty-year-olds rather than the eighteens? But what a pity that your church missed the boat "in order to avoid trouble"!

Neither do I blame the pastor altogether. If he had taken a stand, this same "group of older ladies" would probably have started a movement to oust him. Not all older ladies are like this, thank God.

What, then, is the solution? Some courageous men and women in the church who will provide proper recreation in the church for young people, and stand by a pastor who does something more than preach against the wrong kind of recreation.

Divorced Christian

QUESTION: *Three years ago I joined a church. I know that my sins were all forgiven. The things I once enjoyed I no longer desire. But here is my problem: I was married and divorced. This happened a number of years ago. But every time I hear a radio sermon, or read the Bible, it seems that something comes up about divorce. I get scared half to death and wonder if God will hold my divorce against me. Do you think that my feeling is of the devil? Or is the Lord punishing me?*

ANSWER: I certainly do think that your feeling is of the devil. Man, what kind of a God do you have? Would He forgive you and then ask you to dangle your skeletons before your eyes every day? You are making a great mistake. Remember Lot's wife. Burn your bridges behind you.

Your sin seems to be doubt. Yet, to be perfectly honest, I would judge that you cannot help it. Most people who are chronic worriers about past sins are depressed. Aren't you a pessimist? Don't you expect most people to reject you? Your depression is an emotional problem and needs to be treated as such.

Remember, brother, God has not changed. When He forgives, He forgets. Psalm 103:12: "As far as the east is from the west, so far hath he removed our transgressions from us." Heb. 10:17: "And their sins and iniquities will I remember no more."

Unequally Yoked

QUESTION: *I would like to know if there is any way in which we can justify our country's membership in the United Nations, in view of 1 Corinthians 6:14. Also our treaties with murderers like Tito and Franco.*

ANSWER: The Scripture you refer to has been used to prove many things. It is used to show that a Christian should not marry a non-Christian. That a church member should not go into business with a nonchurch member, and now international relations.

This is a poor way to use God's Word.

What did the verse mean in its setting? What was Paul trying to get across to these Corinthian Christians? To ostracize other people? To be isolationists? To practice religious segregation? No, he was trying to get them to live lives of Christian holiness and integrity, just as our Lord did. "I pray not that thou shouldst take them out of the world, but that thou shouldst keep them from the evil" (John 17:15).

To be "unequally yoked" with unbelievers does not mean not to be yoked at all.

Religion has been greatly hindered by the isolationists and the separationists (the real meaning of the word "Pharisee"). Common sense and Christian love require that we relate ourselves to others, even the bad ones, in the most helpful manner.

Loving Enemies

QUESTION: *The Bible says for us to love our enemies. Does God expect us to love our enemies as much as Jesus did His Father and His disciples? Did Jesus love Judas?*

ANSWER: Yes, Jesus loved Judas. But love is not the same as like, nor the same as friendship. Love is the warm acceptance of a person as he is. We must take people as God gives them to us. There must be interest in, concern for, and appreciation of an individual with all of his distinctive qualities. I admit that it is hard to love those who threaten, or hurt, or dislike us. It is especially hard to love someone who has injured or made us unhappy.

Let's look at it this way. We are placed in a world of persons—children, crooks, hypocrites, saints, and God himself. If we relate ourselves to those who are like us or who help us, we form friendships. If we relate ourselves to a person of the opposite sex about our own age, we have a courtship. But if we relate ourselves in a negative way to other persons, we have war, quarrels, isolation, loneliness, and divisions.

The Christian ideal is community. We need to belong. Only love can join that which belongs together. And love means listening, talking, serving, helping, and being helped. Love is the cement that joins those who have been separated by misunderstanding, difference in temperament, color, or religion.

Where We Go When We Die

QUESTION: *A minister said to me the other day that he believed that when we die our spirit instantly left the body and went to heaven or hell. The question is this: Do you think that anyone who believes that could possibly believe the Bible? It plainly teaches us about the resurrection of the dead, the sea giving up the dead and so forth.*

ANSWER: The minister is right. The saint goes to be with Christ immediately upon the event of death. Christ said, "Today shalt thou be with me in paradise" (Luke 23:43); and in a few moments cried, "Father, into thy hands I commend my spirit" (v. 46). Stephen, breathing his last breath, said, "Lord Jesus, receive my spirit" (Acts 7:59).

The Apostle Paul said that he was "willing rather to be absent from the body, and to be present with the Lord" (2 Cor. 5:8). In the Philippian letter he said that he had "a desire to depart, and to be with Christ; which is far better" (Phil. 1:23).

Side by side with these references is the revelation that we shall all be raised (except those who will be translated) when Christ returns (1 Cor. 15:51 f.; 1 Thess. 4:13–18).

This merely means that when the individual dies, he goes as a person to be with his Lord to await the resurrection of the body at the end of the age. I do not see anything difficult about this, if our Lord chooses to do it that way. Why all the bother? Where do you think the soul stays until the resurrection? In the grave? No, the spirit of a Christian is never separated from his Lord. He is with us while we live, and we go to be with Him when we die.

Are Infants Saved?

QUESTION: *Most of our churches teach that before a child reaches "the age of accountability" he or she is under the blood of Christ and is therefore saved. Where in the Bible is this found? Or is this just taken on reasoning that a child cannot accept or reject Christ before he understands this? How does this square with the Scripture that says that he that believeth not is condemned?*

ANSWER: Do you remember the words of King David when his infant son died? He said, "I shall go to him, but he shall not return to me" (2 Sam. 12:23). This does not throw much light on your question but it does a little. Apparently he felt that the child was safe with God.

No, there is no single passage that can be cited as conclusive proof of the salvation of infants. But do we need any? What kind of God do we have revealed through Jesus Christ? Would He send my child to hell (or even to limbo, whatever that is) for something that Adam did? This is simply preposterous. All we know about God and His ways with man indicate that such a view of God is false and an insult to the Almighty.

You do not need any one passage, not if you know the Father of our Lord Jesus Christ. Let's not insult God by making Him worse than a sadistic criminal.

"He that believeth not" applies to all who have seen the light and rejected it.

Unpardonable Sin

QUESTION: *I am seventeen years old. Last summer in a religious camp I heard about the "unpardonable sin" for the first time. The young preacher said that it was resisting God when He tells you to do something. Ever since I have worried about it. I was converted at ten years of age, and I know that I trusted Christ, but since then I have often failed God.*

ANSWER: What you need to do is talk to some preacher who knows the Bible and does not use it to scare people. Before this idea of your committing the unpardonable sin gets fixed in your mind, seek out some good, sound, sensible pastor and tell him exactly how you feel. He will be able to show that the "unpardonable sin" is not just resisting the will of God, but speaking insultingly of the Spirit with intent to turn others away from God.

People who worry about having committed the unpardonable sin are almost certainly not guilty of it. They wouldn't worry about it if they were hardened enough to commit it. Besides, no Christian will commit the unpardonable sin, because he is kept by the power of God (John 10:27–30; 1 Peter 1:3–5).

If you cannot get rid of your guilty feeling by prayer, consecration, and counsel from a man of God, your problem is more serious. See a good psychiatrist or a psychologist. The time to deal with such guilt complexes is in the early stages.

Prosperous Sinners

QUESTION: *I'm convinced that the sixty-four-dollar question about religion is why people prosper who commit every sin in the book. It seems to me that some of the best people I know seem to have sickness, hardship, poverty, and disappointments.*

ANSWER: Your question is one that has puzzled most thoughtful human beings, and made atheists out of some. So far as I know, there is no answer. Job found no answer. The Psalmist found none, except in humility (Psalm 73). Jeremiah whetted his wits on this very problem (Jer. 5). And Jesus made plain that suffering and handicap are not in proportion to sin (John 9 and Luke 13). The fact is, we do not know.

We may be sure, however, that God knows what He is doing, and that sin will be punished. Perhaps He is being merciful to some, trying to bring them around by goodness. Maybe God does not chastise the devil's children. He may be testing the righteous to bring out their mettle, their witness through suffering. I do not know, but He does.

Your problem is this. You are envious and resentful. All of us get that way at times. Why should we be so concerned about the prosperity of others? Do we not have enough to get by on? Can we afford to question God's providence? There is many a saint who has a very sly envy of the sinners. But the Christian way is best.

Remember, also, that excessive riches need to be controlled by man just as man is learning to control disease, floods, and criminality.

State of the Heathen

QUESTION: *My husband and I believe that if a person should die without ever having heard the Gospel message of salvation, God wouldn't hold him accountable for his sins. Our point is that God is not unjust and if he would condemn a soul to hell for something he didn't know about, that would be unjust. We've been told that we are completely wrong. We would appreciate your answer.*

ANSWER: You are right about God's being just. But you are wrong about his not holding a man accountable for his sins.

A man is condemned for not responding positively to God, which is called "unbelief" in the Bible. That is, he must respond to God as God has made himself known to the individual. Paul says that even the heathen are responsible: "The invisible things of him from the creation of the world are clearly seen, being understood by the things that are made, even his eternal power and Godhead; so that they are without excuse" (Rom. 1:20).

On the other hand, we Christians are responsible for seeing to it that all men hear the Gospel. Their blood is on our hands, in a way. But they are responsible for acting on what light they have. Paul's point is that the heathen have sinned even according to the light they have.

The reason you were told that you were completely wrong was that to say the heathen will be saved without Christ contradicts the Word of God. There is no other name under heaven by which men can be saved except the name of Jesus (Acts 4:12).

Chronic Doubter

QUESTION: *Recently a guest minister preached at our church, and ever since I have had doubts about being born again. I have felt so insecure since I heard this sermon. How does one know when he is born of the Holy Spirit? I don't think everyone has a dramatic experience as did Paul, but I should know in my heart, shouldn't I? I seem to be a chronic doubter.*

ANSWER: Your doubts are not uncommon. They are doubts which many have at one time or another. No two people have the same emotional experience. Take Paul, since you have mentioned him; he had a very dramatic experience. Compare his experience with that of most of the disciples. In many instances, Jesus said, "Come follow me." And they did, believing. These are two extremes, I admit; but who can say that one experience was any more real and effective than the other?

Of course we want to know in our hearts that we are Christians. We ought to know. Our Bible is our source book here. First, we must confess Jesus (Matt. 10:32; Rom. 10:9). Second, we love God and our fellow man (John 13:34–35; 14:21–24; 1 John 3:14). Third, we are led by His Spirit to obey (Rom. 8:9; 1 John 2:3). If we truly believe, God speaks to us through His Word, giving assurance of salvation (1 John 5:10–13).

The one irreducible minimum of Christian experience is repentance and faith. Only you will know whether you have been humble enough to turn to God in simple trust. Let me put it in this way: Are you depending upon Jesus and

His death on the cross as your hope of eternal life? Do you consciously rely upon His accepting love for your peace? Do you believe that God loves you unconditionally and that He will continue to do so? Have you publicly confessed this and do you sincerely try to follow Christ? Then you have nothing to worry about.

Perhaps the sermon was a good one. It caused you to examine the foundations upon which your soul rests. Don't worry about how you feel. Rely upon how God feels about you.

Daughter's Clothes

QUESTION: *I know that the Bible says for a woman not to wear that which pertains to a man. But when my ten-year-old daughter comes to me and says, "Daddy, may I wear jeans to school today?" it is hard for me to know what to say. I think of God and His Word.*

What is the right thing to do? I know that whatever we do will greatly influence others.

ANSWER: The Scripture you refer to about a woman not wearing man's clothing is Deut. 22:5: "The woman shall not wear that which pertaineth unto a man, neither shall a man put on a woman's garment: for all that do so are abomination unto the Lord thy God." It was spoken to the children of Israel about fourteen hundred years before Christ. If we apply these instructions about clothing to our day, we ought also to forbid the plaiting of the hair and the wearing of jewelry (1 Tim. 2:9 and 1 Peter 3:3). This seems to me to be a kind of literalism which has done the cause of Christ a great deal of harm. Christians are to be peculiarly good and useful, not just peculiar.

No, instruction about dress and customs were written to the people of a particular age and country. The principles involved, of wearing clothes which show good religious outlook, is a good one for all time, but each decade has its fads, crazes, and fashions in dress. There are usually no moral or religious issues involved in these. They are simply folk customs.

Let your daughter wear whatever she looks cutest in, provided it is not indiscreet. (I have a twelve-year-old daughter myself.) Don't penalize her because she is religious.

The Bible, as most Christians understand it, does not give any instructions about how long to wear the hair, what length skirts to wear, nor whether to use smearproof lipstick or none.

Suicides

QUESTION: *What consolation can you give the loved ones of those who take their own lives? Are there any Scriptures for this? Are they saved?*

ANSWER: Many people in our society are faced with your problem. Every year in the United States between fifteen thousand and twenty thousand people commit suicide—this is more than the number of homicides. Suicide ranks ninth among the causes of death. Many of these are professing Christians, and some are even church leaders. This tragedy is not rare.

Yes, I can give you some consolation. There is the same

consolation that there is for the loved ones of any other deceased person. If a person is a Christian, he goes to be with the Savior when he dies. His sins are under the blood. He is saved by grace through faith, not by works.

Scriptures? Yes, many of them. Start with John 3:16: "For God so loved the world, that he gave his only begotten Son, that whosoever believeth in him should not perish, but have everlasting life." 1 John 1:7 says that the blood of Jesus Christ cleanses from *all* sin. Jesus himself promised that those who believe in him possess eternal life and shall not come into condemnation (John 5:24; 10:27–30). If we take Christ at his word we must believe in the security of the true believers.

Now some will say that if a person takes his own life, he is not a true believer. Who can say that? How can we say that this sin is greater than another? Many people who destroy themselves are mentally ill, therefore not morally responsible. In that case there is no sin at all.

The idea that suicides go to hell is a Roman Catholic doctrine, not a New Testament teaching. Catholics say that suicide is a "mortal" sin for which you cannot be forgiven, because the person dies before the last saving rites could be administered. Others think that the person could not have been saved because that sin could not have been confessed to God. The Bible knows nothing of these human theories.

Evolution

QUESTION: *What are your views on "The Theory of Evolution"? Recently I have been reading that many of the leaders in various religious groups have stated that there is not so much conflict between this theory and the Bible as was once thought.*

Do you think the Bible should be taken figuratively or literally? It seems to me that you couldn't take it figuratively and have any peace or conviction at all.

ANSWER: If you want a good philosophical discussion of this subject, I refer you to *Introduction to the Philosophy of Religion* (1951) by Professor Bertocci of Boston University.

I suppose there has been more hate and ignorance tied up with the fight over evolution than any subject that has entertained (?) the mind of modern man. We all seem to want to "damn" somebody over the question. A little humility on the part of all of us might help.

Here are the facts, as I see them. Life came into being on this planet at a time not too clearly discernible, in a way that is a complete mystery. The Bible says that "In the beginning God created the heaven and the earth . . . And the Lord God formed man of the ground, and breathed into his nostrils the breath of life." I believe this without any question.

If scientists can tell us how the creative process took place, it is all right with me. But when they talk of its occurring by "chance" that just means "it occurred I know not how or why."

I may be simple, but the great scientists I have read all come to a "missing link" or a jumping-off place. Right there is where my faith comes in to supply the answers. The Bible does not tell us how God created. I personally don't think the scientists know, either. I take the Bible seriously, some of it literally and some of it figuratively.

Are Jews God's Favorites?

QUESTION: *Do you think that the Jews are still God's chosen people?*

Our pastor says because the Jews have rejected Christ, God has now turned His back upon them, and they mean no more to Him than anyone else who has rejected Christ.

ANSWER: There are many people who teach that the Jews are still God's chosen people, and that He is showing special favor to them in the modern Zionist movement. I do not believe this, but I do not care to engage in controversy about the matter.

Matthew 21:43 says: "The kingdom of God shall be taken from you and given to a nation bringing forth the fruits thereof." Peter, a Jew, said in the house of Cornelius, "Of a truth I perceive that God is no respecter of persons; But in every nation he that feareth him, and worketh righteousness, is accepted with him" (Acts 10:34–35). The phrase, "respecter of persons" means that He shows no partiality: all are alike before Him. This is the New Testament revelation.

Paul makes plain in Galatians that Christians are the true children of the Abrahamic covenant. "There is neither Jew nor Greek, there is neither bond nor free, there is neither male nor female: for ye are all one in Christ Jesus. And if ye be Christ's, then are ye Abraham's seed, and heirs according to the promise" (Gal. 3:28–29).

There is your answer, plain as day.

◈ CHURCH PROBLEMS

Church Picture Stolen

QUESTION: *A young lady in our church was gloriously saved after seeking salvation for some time. Later she presented the church with a beautiful picture of Christ. Quite a few things were said and done concerning the picture, but just this past week the picture was taken from off the walls of the church and its whereabouts are not known. The young lady is a babe in Christ and is deeply hurt.*

Can you help us (the church) to locate the picture?

ANSWER: No, I'm afraid I can't help you locate the picture. But I can help you to help the young lady—that is your real problem.

The picture was stolen, likely, by some church member who thought that he would stop the controversy. There are a good many Christians (I happen to be one) who dislike seeing pictures of Christ hanging on the walls of church auditoriums. They seem so inadequate.

Now that the picture is stolen, what should the real Christians do? Return evil for evil? Stir up more trouble by replacing it? I think not. This is one theft that may have been a blessing. (Understand, I don't advise evil to get good results.)

Some mature church members ought to sit down with this new convert and help her to see that nobody intended to insult her. Even good people make serious mistakes. This is her chance to grow. Pray with her and talk it out with her. If she lets this cripple her, she wouldn't get far in the Christian life, anyway. Troubles will come; they must be overcome.

Tithing Problem

QUESTION: *My husband and I have a small business and we are still in debt for it. We try to make our payments and keep our children in school. However, we have never paid ourselves a salary, therefore we don't know how we are supposed to tithe.*

Our problem is twofold: How are we to compute our tithe? And should we put it all through the church? We also donate to Red Cross and other causes.

ANSWER: Your second question is an easy one. Of course, your tithe should be put through the church. It is not yours to use as you see fit. "The tithe is the Lord's." You have no more right to control it than you have to withhold it. A New Testament church treasury is the place for a Christian's tithe.

Now about figuring the tithe. You must know about how much you are taking out of your business to live on. If you do not, Uncle Sam may have you before a judge before long. It seems to me that what you are taking out of business to live on is your personal income. Give a tenth of that.

Be thoroughly conscientious in estimating your tithe, and

the Lord will bless you—spiritually especially. It is a good feeling to know that you are being honest with God.

And remember, you cannot outgive God. So where there is a question, give the Lord the benefit of the doubt.

Women in the Church

QUESTION: *Do you think it is wrong for women to work in the church? If they did not, sometimes we could not have a Sunday school, as there are very few men who will lead in our church.*

Some of our members quote 1 Tim. 2:12–15 and 1 Cor. 14:34–35. Does this apply today?

ANSWER: The principle applies today but there is a general opinion that the status of women was very different in New Testament days from our day. The principle is stated in 1 Tim. 2:10, that women are to dress and behave as "becometh women professing godliness." Paul was not trying to lay down rules for all women of all time, but for those in that particular culture.

In Galatians (3:28) Paul stated that there is "neither male nor female: for all are one in Christ Jesus." Apparently he meant that there was no discrimination in the church.

This old question of feminism has been kicked around for the last hundred years, especially as women have grown in their freedom. Surely the church does not wish to be the last to accept women on equal level and status with men.

On the other hand, men are the natural leaders, and both men and women are usually happiest when men assume their rightful place. Women can probably do their best service by pushing the men forward in church work. But to quote a verse here and there in the New Testament is a poor way to arrive at present-day Christian procedures in this field.

Bad Housekeeping

QUESTION: *Among our members is a woman who is always the first to offer to do anything that needs to be done. She is faithful and dependable. We appreciate her good qualities, but she is the world's worst housekeeper.*

She sometimes furnishes food for our church suppers and works in the kitchen, and we shudder to think of eating anything she prepares. What can we do? Before they eat, people are asking which dishes Mrs. "X" brought.

ANSWER: Mrs. "X" is a problem, and many churches have a Mrs. "X." Filth is inexcusable, and I can understand how you and the other church members feel.

Try "organizing" her out of the kitchen. The habit of depending on volunteers is a dangerous one under some circumstances. If certain ones were selected for specific tasks and hers could be something besides food, that might help the situation.

Perhaps you could get a group of women together, including her, and have a talk by the county health nurse or demonstration agent on cleanliness and food. You might even have some courses on this in connection with your church.

In rare cases, some woman in the church might have talent or tact enough to talk this over with Mrs. "X," but this is rare indeed and might lead to injury.

"Cleanliness is next to godliness," John Wesley said.

But after all, we cannot afford to hurt a fine person like Mrs. "X" unless it is necessary. It may be that your group can tolerate some deviation from their high standard for the sake of "one for whom Christ died."

Money for All Causes

QUESTION: *The majority of our members in the small rural church to which I belong are poor and renters. One rich spinster controls our church and encourages members to send their money to foreign missions, radio and TV religious programs and to all sort of things—anything but their local church. We need a new church building and our own pastor is underpaid. This spinster says that local expenses should be met by free-will offerings instead of the system of tithes plus offerings. What can we do?*

ANSWER: If you are telling the truth about your church, it is a strange institution. Most churches want to spend most of their money on local expenses and let foreign missions take the leftovers.

The rich spinster needs to use a microscope as well as a telescope. She is farsighted and needs a new pair of spectacles. The rich as well as the poor ought to put their offerings, as well as their tithes, into the local church treasury. Then a budget can be worked out that will include both local needs and foreign needs.

God has one institution for supporting his work—a New Testament church. It is the duty of every pastor and Sunday school teacher to teach storehouse tithing. This, and this alone, will solve the local and foreign-mission problems.

What can you do? Teach. Talk. Pray. Work. Error can be overcome by truth.

Nominating Committee Unkind

QUESTION: *The Nominating Committee of our church has hurt many people very deeply by dropping from their recommendations some who have served for many years in a particular job. Wouldn't it be kinder to speak to them in Christian love and appreciation rather than dropping them without saying a word?*

ANSWER: Our churches have a real problem at this point. Jobs have to be passed around in order to develop all of the good people. If the Nominating Committee tells the individual that he is being relieved of a job before they present his name to the church, he may start an insurrection in order to hold the office. Or the church may not accept the nomination, which would make the Committee look premature or presumptuous in speaking to the outgoing individual.

I believe that the solution lies in training the church member not to expect or seek an office at any time, and to trust the Nominating Committee to follow the Holy Spirit's leadership. After all, the purpose of such a committee is to work prayerfully through the whole church roll and choose the best people for all jobs—"best" in the sense of doing the best for the cause of Christ.

An I-bruise-easy attitude just won't work in a church. You have to be humble and tough-minded.

"Shelved" Members

QUESTION: *At what age or under what conditions should the workers in our churches be "shelved" or denied the privilege of active service that they have prepared themselves for? The young people seem to be taking over the church, while the gray heads who have had the study courses, the clinics, and so forth, are set aside as too old.*

ANSWER: Your question points up a serious problem. We will soon have from fifteen to twenty million people in America above sixty-five. These older people can be one of our churches' greatest strengths. And many of them deserve more attention and respect and leadership than they get.

They, the older ones, need to be very patient with us younger ones while together we are learning how to keep on using them. Twenty-five years ago we preachers were taught in the seminaries how to provide a church program for young people. The seminaries are just now waking up to this new problem of "later maturity."

In the meantime, let the younger people lead. You led when you were young. Remember that holding offices does not constitute all of Christian work. Don't fade away, fire up! Do the visiting, the giving, the talking for good, the praying. Let the young voices sing in the choir. Let the middle-aged men teach the junior boys and serve as deacons.

If you do this, you will stay off the shelf, and the church will go forward.

Too Sick to Fight

QUESTION: *How can a person go to church to worship in spirit and truth when the pastor isn't truthful? You know he does not live as a pastor should. He wants to be a dictator in everything. He hurts people and seems to have no regard for their feelings.*

Can we get help in any way to make him resign? I have been sick a lot, and this church mess breaks my heart.

ANSWER: Once in a long while an unworthy pastor gets into a church. Of course, all of us are deficient in some ways. If your situation is as critical as it seems, I'd do an awful lot of praying. More than once the Bible tells of people who "fell on their faces" before God when a crisis came.

The most important thing is that the church stick together. They will be there after the pastor is gone.

Yes, a congregation can force a pastor to resign, just as they call him to be their pastor. They can declare the pulpit "vacant"—sometimes it is rather vacant anyway. But forcing a resignation is a pretty drastic measure and nearly always does more harm than good. I'd pray a long time before I would have part in such a measure.

As for going to church to worship, don't let the perversity of man keep you from serving God. Ask God to take all ill will out of your heart and be patient. And let the well people do the church fighting; it's no job for a sick person.

New Version

QUESTION: *My church has split over the Revised Standard Version of the Bible. When the new literature came out with the picture of the new version on the back of one of the quarterlies, our church went wild and voted out the whole Training Union literature. Our pastor led in the movement, and the church voted not to send any more mission money.*

Many have already left. Should I get my letter and go to another church? I am associational Training Union director, so it puts me on quite a spot.

ANSWER: God must be long-suffering to put up with His churches. It is nothing short of a tragedy that churches quarrel over which translation to read, while the unchurched do not read any. But as Dr. J. D. Grey has brilliantly said, "They used to burn the translators, but now they only burn the translations."

No, I don't think I would leave. That is, if God gives you the grace to stay. Only religion can reform religion; and if you stay and love these people, the next pastor may lead them back into a humble, reasonable path. Personally, I do not subscribe to any one version of the Bible. God speaks to me through many of them—even the new versions—and I try to follow Him. That seems to me more important than fighting someone who disagrees with me.

Pastor Won't Pay Bills

QUESTION: *What are you going to do with a pastor who just will not pay his debts? Now don't tell us that we are not paying him enough. He is making more than the average family of his congregation. We recently raised his salary, and one man paid some of his debts for him. He spends money on TV sets, cold drinks, and other luxuries, and lets his bills go unpaid. It is hurting the cause of Christ. What can we do?*

ANSWER: Just such a case came to my knowledge recently, and I will tell you how it was solved.

This was a fine pastor, a good preacher, but a sorry financier. After some of the members began to gossip about the matter, a fine young deacon, about the age of the pastor, went to see him about it. He assured him that he was not trying to criticize him. He talked over his financial problems with him. They worked out a budget together. The deacon took some cash which the pastor had on hand and paid some pressing bills. The deacon gave him counsel on the meeting of future bills. They agreed on further stated interviews about the matter. Real improvement was made.

This makes sense to me. After all, every pastor has some weaknesses. And he does not have a pastor. If some member of the church could be a real Christian brother to him, it might help an otherwise passive individual.

Choir Members

QUESTION: *Should a choir director have complete authority as to whom he should invite to sing in the choir? Or is it proper for some of the women singers to dictate to him as to whom he should invite, even if they do not read music?*

ANSWER: This is a very ticklish question. Choirs have been notoriously known as the "war department" of the church.

When a church elects a choir director or minister of music, he should be given complete authority for screening choir members. If he is not competent, he should not be elected. If he is, the church should trust his musical knowledge and spiritual tact.

Nearly every choir has one or two people in it who are troublemakers. They set themselves up as authorities on repertoire, on interpretation, and even on tonal quality. God pity the poor choir directors who do not have the loyalty of the congregation.

If a church is to have the kind of music that the Lord's service deserves, it needs trained people, consecrated people, and people mature enough to work together. The aim of beauty and praise to God should come first. This requires the kind of unselfishness that is quite a strain on small souls.

Every community I know has enough native talent to have great church music. And the church deserves the finest music. But only training and consecration will bring this about.

Using First Names

QUESTION: *What do you think of the growing custom of calling ministers (and members of the church) by their first names?*

Recently we met a lady whose church had changed pastors lately. When being asked who her pastor was, she said, "I can't remember his last name, but his first name is Joe. That's what they call him."

ANSWER: Your question has a lot of overtones. Friendliness and informality and frankness are so close to Christian love that I feel you are dealing with an important issue. Such issues should be settled, not by quoting a verse or two of Scripture, but by thinking of the Christian spirit.

Personally I prefer to be called Brother. I don't like Reverend; and Doctor (which I am usually called) sounds as bad. But I seldom mention these matters. Titles such as these are merely handles determined largely by custom.

The questions to ask, in order to settle this issue, are: Does the custom (first names or otherwise) make for closeness and warmth? Does it give a sense of brotherliness and equality? At the same time, does it make for respect, especially with regard to the minister?

In the New Testament first names seem to have been used almost universally. Sometimes the term "Brother" was added, as in Acts 9:17. But that was a long time ago and customs were different.

I would say that using first names is a good thing generally, but ministers ought to be addressed in public by the title of Brother, Mister, Pastor, or whatever term seems right for the area.

Can't Go to Church

QUESTION: *I have a certain illness which causes me such embarrassment that at times I feel like covering my face and hiding. I do my best not to let it worry me, because I cannot help it.*

I listen to messages by radio and desire to go to church as much as anyone. I have been saved and try to live the Christian life. Will not my life be a successful one?

ANSWER: Success for the Christian is finding God's will for his life, and living in it. You have a unique path to walk, just as each life has. Do not measure your success by God's will for others. I judge that your trouble is epilepsy or some serious deformity. Why are you ashamed of it, whatever it is?

If you would go to church, you have no idea how much encouragement you might be to others who have handicaps also. The trouble with you is that you have labeled yourself as some sort of shameful person. A person is always precious in God's sight, and in the sight of true Christians. A person who has epileptic seizures, for example, is not an "epileptic," but a person who happens to have epilepsy. Is that any greater disgrace than having diabetes or heart trouble or undulant fever?

It will do the church good to enter into "the fellowship of suffering." Christian fellowship is one of the divinely ordained means of growth. Without it you cannot be your best for Christ.

Why don't you call a pastor and talk the whole thing over with him? He will probably understand. God does, and loves you as dearly as any of his children.

Blames Preacher for Marriage

QUESTION: *What is your opinion of a preacher who would perform the marriage ceremony of a knowingly secret marriage of a couple, both of whom have not finished high school? The girl graduates from high school in three months, and the boy will then go into the army. Don't you think that he should have counseled these children or advised their parents, as all live in the same neighborhood?*

ANSWER: It sounds to me as if you are picking on this preacher. Have you heard his side of the story? How do you know that he did not counsel the "children," as you call them? Most preachers do.

As for advising the parents, I can imagine what that would have brought about. These young people would have taken off to the adjoining county, been married by a justice of the peace, and never confided in a preacher again as long as they lived.

Counseling people does not mean telling them what they ought or ought not to do. It means to help individuals to understand what they are doing, and why they are doing it, so that they may make more intelligent decisions. Preachers who play God are just as wrong as psychiatrists or parents or judges who play God.

It sounds as if the couple getting married started out with two strikes against them. Perhaps you, the community, and the preacher combined, may help them grow a good marriage in spite of the handicaps.

Deacon's Wife

QUESTION: *What can or ought to be done about a deacon's wife who tries to run or boss every little thing from the election of officers to the calling of the pastor? She gossips and attends to everybody's business but her own, regardless of whom it hurts or mixes up.*

ANSWER: There is one in every church. That is, one person, not always a deacon's wife, who is never satisfied unless she is controlling other people. This is a dictator in church member's clothing. Beware!

Democracy is a rare achievement. It survives only where those who believe in it understand how it is undermined. It thrives only when all of the cards are kept on the top of the table, when majority rule is insisted on and accepted, when love and respect for each person are sponsored.

Dictatorship thrives in an environment of conniving, working up secretly a vote for a particular issue, threatening those who disagree by name-calling, and in allowing deceptive methods to be tolerated.

What can be done about this woman? Grow some church members who are too mature to fall for such domination. There is no other solution.

Treasurer Refuses

QUESTION: *Ours is a small rural church with two treasurers. The building-fund treasurer refuses to make a report of how much money is in the building fund. He says that it is nobody's business who gives and how much. What can the church do?*

ANSWER: There is something badly wrong with your treasurer, perhaps something wrong with his judgment or training. All officers of a church are servants of the church, not dictators.

I would stand up in a business meeting of my church and say, "Brother Moderator, I don't want what I have to say to be misunderstood. I love every one of my brothers and sisters in Christ. My motion is not a reflection on anyone's character. I suspect no one, believe me, but it is not fair to anyone to be asked to handle money without the protection of the presence of others at the handling of money, and without all the facts regarding the money being known to the whole church. I move, sir, that hereafter we ask for regular reports (monthly or quarterly) from both treasurers and that we have all checks signed by at least two people in our church. This is for the protection of everybody concerned and for the sake of a sound financial policy in our church. If we ask people to sacrifice in giving, we must be good stewards of every cent they give. This is a church matter and we are responsible to God for the manner in which these details are handled." Some such motion.

If this does not get the job done, resort to prayer, persuasion, and any other method that is in accord with Christian love and respect.

Scared Church Member

QUESTION: *My pastor has asked me to teach a Sunday school class, and I would like to do it, but fear seems to overcome me. It is the same way when I am called on to lead in public prayer.*

Can anything be done about my fear? I am thirty-eight years old and wonder if there is any hope for me to change. This is not just stage fright. I get butterflies in my stomach and shake all over.

ANSWER: Fear is not anything to be ashamed of. It has to be lived with. The chances are that you could master a part of it if you did not feel, as most people do, that only cowards are afraid.

Surely you can overcome it, enough to serve. Why don't you try doing more in Brotherhood or other church groups. That is one of the things that they are for. If I were you, I would promise the Lord, and perhaps my pastor, that, fear or no fear, I would do my duty. When you are called upon to lead in prayer, stumble around and do the best that you can. Never say, "Excuse me, please." And about teaching, prepare well, pray calmly but often, do the best you can, and you may in time win. Sometimes we have to swallow our pride in order to be our best.

Don't run and don't avoid the painful situation. The butterflies will quit fluttering when they find out that it does no good to flutter. Stand till you fall.

Pagan Christmas

QUESTION: *Why is it that there is so much emphasis on Santa Claus, Christmas trees, and so on, instead of the real meaning of Christmas? It seems to me that we have about forgotten that it is the celebration of the birth of Christ.*

ANSWER: You are exactly right. Christmas is for many people a time of drinking, eating, swapping presents, and generally forgetting God.

For example, right here in Kansas City a woman was standing outside a store window looking at a beautiful manger scene. She was overheard to say, "Well, I declare; just look at that. It looks as if religion is just crowding Christmas clear out of everything. No Santa Claus nor nothing in there. Religion is sure crowding Christmas out."

On the other hand, millions of Christians are really thinking about our wonderful Savior at this season. Many will read the second chapter of Luke again. Many churches have special offerings for worthy causes, such as foreign missions, at Christmas time. There are plenty of causes if you really want to put Christ back in Christmas.

What is happening is that Christians are getting more Christian and pagans are getting more pagan.

Santa Claus

QUESTION: *I have been asked to serve on the Christmas program committee for our church. The other members of this committee want to include "Santa Claus" readings and have "Santa Claus" hand out the treats.*

How do you feel about such a program?

ANSWER: Santa Claus has been a problem to many Christians. Some people do not allow their children to believe the myth about him and his reindeer, big fat belly, and the rest of it. Others think of the story as a beautiful fiction embodying the spirit of giving.

Personally, I can't remember ever believing in Santa Claus. I'm sure I did, but the whole matter was treated with humor by my Christian parents. They talked about the old fellow but we never cleaned the chimney for him.

I do not see any great objection to using Santa Claus readings and having a "real" Santa Claus hand out the treats. It's all in fun and in good will. There is danger, however, that in some churches and homes Santa Claus has stolen the show from Christ. We who are over six years of age ought to put Christ back in the center of the stage. After all, it is His birthday.

Happy Young People

QUESTION: *Our pastor takes our young people out for a good time. He seems to think that all they need is to play. What they do is not so bad, I guess, but a lot of us older ones who are paying the bills don't believe in it. Do you think that Jesus meant for people to have a good time?*

ANSWER: I certainly do. I am reminded of the editor who was asked if he believed Jesus ever laughed. He said, "I don't know whether or not He did, but He fixed me up so that I could."

You older people in your church ought to re-examine your position. You played when you were young. And if you would play more now, there would be fewer doctor bills to pay. Playing is a part of life, as well as praying. The church is in a pretty sorry position when it criticizes young people for the wrong kind of recreation and offers them no substitutes.

You must have a fine pastor. Most pastors get so busy about strictly spiritual matters that they neglect the well-rounded life. A strong church must funnel many of life's activities through its program.

For heaven's sake, do not take sides with some sour-pusses in the church. There are some kill-joys in every congregation. Back your pastor and trust him to lead your young people.

Baptist Bridge

QUESTION: *I am a minister, pastor of a Baptist church. We have never allowed any kind of cards in our home. Now my fourteen-year-old son is playing Rook in the home of one of our members. My son is a Christian, takes an active part in the church, and I have led the church to establish a good recreation program. The question is, should I try to stop my boy from playing Rook or let him play at my home as the other boys' parents do?*

ANSWER: You are writing to a Rook shark, or I used to be. I was reared in the home of a Baptist deacon in Tennessee where Rook was our sole card game. We played it by the hour. We called it "Baptist bridge." Somehow I never ran across the idea that it was wrong until after I was grown. I could name you (but I won't) a half-dozen of the leading pastors in the South who play Rook regularly and often have a game after sessions at convention meetings.

I never even heard of anyone gambling on Rook. Did you? I suppose there are some; they gamble on dominoes, football, baseball, and nearly everything else. But recreation of the wholesome sort is necessary to a well-balanced life. I do not have as much time for recreation now as in former years, but I believe in it.

Personally, I think you are dead wrong. It seems to me that your son ought to be encouraged to play Rook right in your own home. I know some people will protest against this viewpoint, but when I get older, if Rook has not completely gone out of style, I intend to play again.

Song-Title Sermons

QUESTION: *What do you think of the practice of using popular song titles as the title of sermons? Our pastor often does this, and it seems to me to cheapen his preaching.*

ANSWER: It seems to me that the real question is which song titles he used and what he made out of them.

Preaching is serious business but it does not need to be somber or sad.

After all, the title of a sermon need not tell you all that the sermon is about. It is rather an attention-getter, and should point in the direction of the theme.

Two of the best church members I know came to my church for the first time when they read in the newspaper that I was preaching on "Cross Over the Bridge." It was a sermon on the importance of decision. They were both deeply convinced and later joined the church.

I wouldn't preach on "The Purple People Eater" but I might use "Love Is a Many-Splendored Thing."

There is so much drabness and mediocrity in church service, for heaven's sake don't discourage preachers who use attractive sermon titles. The average publisher would not think of using a manuscript which has as little imagination in its title as the average sermon title has.

There is such a thing as being interesting without being cheap.

Clique in Church

QUESTION: *We have in our church a little group of people who are not faithful, but for several years, when time comes to elect officers they always show up and vote for each other. This year the nominating committee (a fine, spiritual group) decided to replace these people. Then, led by one woman, they nominated from the floor, and got people there who never came any other time. The meeting was bedlam.*

My heart is broken. What are we to do? We have lost three preachers in seven years over this situation.

ANSWER: You say that "a little group" did so-and-so. If they are so small, how did they get the people elected from the floor? Where were the rest of you while they were beating the bushes to get their side out? A church is controlled by the majority of the people who are aggressive enough to get to the business meeting. I don't blame the preachers for leaving if you who believe in democracy are too lazy to get out to business meeting.

The Bible tells us what to do about people who form themselves into a clique. "As for a man who is factious, after admonishing him once or twice, have nothing more to do with him, knowing that such a person is perverted and sinful; he is self-condemned" (Titus 3:10–11 RSV). And Paul said to the Christians at Corinth that "there must be factions among you in order that those who are genuine among you may be recognized" (1 Cor. 11:19 RSV).

Real Christians do not join cliques!

Anonymous Letters

QUESTION: *There is one person (possibly more) in our church who writes anonymous letters. She (or he) writes them to the pastor, the choir director, the Sunday school superintendent and the Lord only knows who else. They are the vilest things you ever read, full of criticism and ugliness. What can the church do about such people? And what should our attitude be toward such behavior?*

ANSWER: If these letters contain vulgarity or accusations that are criminal (such as slander) the post office and the Federal Bureau of Investigation will deal with them. If not, as is usually the case, the best thing to do is ignore them.

I know a pastor who never allows his secretary to show him an anonymous letter. Some studious soul really gets cheated in his case, for this pastor gets plenty. Most pastors receive such letters sooner or later.

It is hard to say the truth about such letter writers. Some say that they are among the meanest people on earth. Others say that they are sick mentally. Still others say that they are fearful cowards. Only God knows, so let Him judge them.

This much is reasonably certain. They are not hard to spot. You can submit these anonymous letters to any group in your community and ask them who would write such stuff. The same one or two names will come up as the guilty ones. To me this shows that, sick or sinful, these people are different. They mean to be.

Ignore them. Life is too short to spend time on people who won't sign their names.

Why So Critical?

QUESTION: *Why are so many church people so hard on sinners?*

Here is an example. A man whom I have known, a leader in our church, made a mistake. It was found out. What did the church people do? They gossiped about him, criticized him, and consigned him to the lower regions. To my knowledge not a one of them went to him as a brother. Is this the way Christians should act?

ANSWER: There are two kinds of sinners in this world. Those who violate the laws of God and man, and those who kill the violators. The Prodigal Son and the Elder Brother (Luke 15) are two good examples. Of course, actually, we are all sinners, some saved by grace and others who have not been saved.

I know what you mean. There are people in the church who judge others, who gossip and criticize. All of us regret this. But I honestly believe that there are more merciful, kindly, understanding people in the church than anywhere else on earth. I know them. They are the church within the church.

Are you a church man? Did you go to the erring man and

try to show him some Christian friendship? If your church leader who has gone astray ever needed a friend, it is now.

Don't be too hard on church people. They are human too. Get in the middle of the church and love, instead of criticizing. Only religion can reform religion.

When Converted

QUESTION: *Our pastor said that he was brought up in a church, attended regularly, and did not know when he was saved.*

My experience has been different. I remember the time and place. What is your experience in this matter?

ANSWER: I remember precisely when I received Christ as my Savior. It was an overwhelming, life-changing, dramatic experience.

But the human memory is very tricky. Many people who have received Christ, show real evidence of conversion, are trusting wholly in His grace, do not remember the time, place, or feeling connected with their salvation. The important thing to remember is not the point of conversion but the fact. We are not converted in our sleep. We must consciously commit ourselves to Christ, renounce our self-dependence, and rely upon Him as Savior and Lord.

A friend of mine argues that he believes in capital punishment but does not remember when he began believing in it. But conversion is not an intellectual belief. It is commitment, repentance, trust.

Emotional experiences of conversion will vary widely from person to person, but it must be at a given point in time.

Your pastor may not remember, but if he is saved, it occurred at one time and at one place.

Forgiving Enemy

QUESTION: *One whom we all loved and trusted as a true friend did a great wrong to a member of our family. I know the Christian way is to forgive. I think I have forgiven him until I think I may meet him. Then I avoid him if I can. If I cannot, I feel "panicky"—so I realize I must not have forgiven him yet.*

How can one compel oneself to forgive? I speak well of him if the occasion arises, but the old hurt remains so deep that I can't overcome it.

ANSWER: I'm not at all sure that you have not forgiven. Your "panicky" feeling may be the result of fear or of just plain conditioning—a cat will not sit down on a cold stove because of "conditioning."

If you feel, however, that you have not forgiven the wrong, you might try this: Every time the image of the man comes to your mind, think of some good quality he has. Just keep looking for them and adding one after another of his good deeds or traits. Or try praying for specific blessings for him. Not just "God bless John," or whatever his name is, but ask for specific good things to come into his life, and keep on until you feel no unforgiveness. When you are near him, pray for him.

And do not worry about the feeling aspect of forgiveness. There are some unconscious factors working there. You can't change that.

Pray for your own heart. Only the power of God can overcome human hate. Cast yourself on His mercy and depend upon His grace.

Plagued by Doubts

QUESTION: *I have recurring doubts about my salvation. There are times when I feel the Lord's love and presence, but the times when I doubt, usually after reading something explaining salvation in detail, are a horror. It even causes physical nausea and almost paralyzes me.*

How can I know for certain that I am saved?

ANSWER: Individuals who have never been plagued by such doubts will never understand you. They will insert a coin Scripture into the slot of your mind and expect you to hit the jackpot of assurance.

Assurance, which is your need, is hard for some people. I have three suggestions. First, realize that your salvation rests upon a person. As Martin Luther said, "Let Him who died for my soul see to the saving of it." God is love. He does not change just because you have mood swings. Drop a rock into a clear pool which reflects the moon and it will appear that the moon is shattered. But it hasn't been. The moon, like God, stays the same. Read 1 John 3:20.

Second, rely upon the promises of God. They are plain, concerning salvation. If you trust God to do what He has promised to do, the best you know how, God does the rest. Read John 1:12; 3:16; and Romans 10:9-10; and 1 John 5:10-13.

Finally, obedience brings assurance. Read John 7:17 and 1 John 2:3; 3:24. If you have an unreasonable conscience, your inner demands will be absurd. No one can feel secure with a tyrannical conscience. But prompt obedience, action instead of dreams and hopes, will bring about assurance as spring rains bring up the flowers.

God understands your doubts and does not blame you.

Answering God's Call

QUESTION: *When I was a young man I felt the call to preach. At least, I thought I did. Through the years I have been a salesman and very successful, but I have felt guilty over not preaching. Now I am fifty. What can I do at this age? I am active in my church. I even do some talking to people about Christ. But I don't preach.*

ANSWER: Finding God's will is not as simple as some people make it sound. We look for a "program" which will tell us what we will be doing ten years from now. Or we seek absolute certainty. Remember that we were ordained to walk by faith (2 Cor. 5:7).

It seems to me that the only right thing for you to do is to follow the leadership of God's Spirit. I mean, follow it *today*, each day. You seem to feel that because God called you years ago, or you felt that He did, that He is not on speaking terms with you now. On the other hand, your own usefulness in the church seems to indicate that He has used you.

Often God accepts our second best. None of us follows His will perfectly. Yet if we are willing, we may find His will from day to day.

There are other ways of preaching besides "sermons in a pulpit." Do you support and help your pastor? Would you preach the best you can if the Lord tells you to? Are you making your money and your daily life count for Christ? You cannot make up for the past, but you can live for Christ in the present.

Seduced by Church Worker

QUESTION: *I have been extremely active in church work since I joined at twelve. I am now twenty-four.*

A leader in our church, also very active, and twice my age, began to make advances to me, and I fell for it. We had intimate relations. Now I am in love with a fine Christian boy my own age. Even though I have broken with the older man, I have several problems about this. Should I tell the church and expose this man? Do you think God will forgive me of my sinful past? And should I tell my sordid story to this boy I am going with now? Please answer as soon as possible.

ANSWER: You certainly do have problems. Your biggest one is finding why you are so insecure that you would be immoral in order to get through to someone. This is an emotional problem and needs treatment.

Of course God will forgive you if you have truly repented. "The blood of Jesus Christ his Son cleanseth us from all sin" (1 John 1:7).

No, I would not tell the church. You were not really seduced. I very strongly suspect that you gave this man some "come hither" looks and words. You were old enough to know better.

Now about the boy friend, I don't know what to tell you about this. Honesty is necessary to a good relationship. I would decide this on the basis of what telling this particular boy would do to him. Some men feel very strongly about such matters. He just might find this out after marriage and be very disturbed. Ordinarily, I would advise against confessions. This is primarily between you and your God.

Judged by Heart or Mind?

QUESTION: *My question is, will Jesus judge us by what is in our hearts, or what is in our minds? I know that many things go through my mind that have never been in my heart.*

ANSWER: What is inside us of thoughts or feelings are very complex and obscure. We do not even know how to judge ourselves, much less our neighbors. So far as the distinction between heart and mind, I am not so certain.

If you mean, will God blame us for thoughts or feelings that we cannot avoid, I would say, no. The birds fly over our heads, but we are responsible if they build nests in our hair.

Paul wrote of "the day when God shall judge the secrets of men by Jesus Christ according to my gospel" (Rom. 2:16). And, of course, we know that God looks on the heart and not the outward appearance of men.

In every heart, saved or unsaved, there sits some fear, doubt, lust, pride, and hate. But there are also trust, humility, love, and desire to obey in the saved heart.

Yes, God will judge our motives and our secret thoughts. But in Jesus Christ we are safe. Those who believe "shall not come into condemnation." This is our hope, our only hope.

Tempted to Sin

QUESTION: *Can a Christian be tempted to sin and still be a Christian? I wanted to have an affair with a woman but resisted the temptation. I know that Jesus said that "whosoever looketh on a woman to lust after her hath committed adultery with her already in his heart." What did he mean by this? Is it just as bad to think evil as it is to do evil?*

ANSWER: Of course it is not as bad to think evil as it is to do it. This is pure bosh and needs to be revised. Jesus nowhere says that the thought is just as bad as the act.

What Jesus was trying to help us to see was that the lustful thought precedes the lustful act. Man's temptations are inside himself. James said, "Every man is tempted when he is drawn away of his own lust, and enticed" (Jas. 1:14). Every person is tempted. The proof that he is on God's side is that he resists temptation. Otherwise we become bellhops to our own passions.

The fact that you thought of having an affair with this woman does not prove that you are not a Christian. The question is, what did you do with these thoughts? Did you give the consent of your mind to go ahead? Or did you turn your thoughts completely to better things? This is what Jesus would have done.

The Epistle to the Hebrews says that Jesus "was in all points tempted like as we are, yet without sin" (Heb. 4:15). If Christ was tempted, we should not expect to avoid it ourselves.

Most people think of doing wrong, but the Christian resists the thought and proceeds to find some way to channel his energies in constructive activity.

140

Cruel Criticism

QUESTION: *Good Christians show a wonderful attitude toward sinners whom they are trying to win to the Lord. Why do they sometimes direct the most cruel kind of criticism toward each other?*

ANSWER: I have often wondered the same thing. I guess it is for the same reason that we criticize the critics. Intolerance of intolerance is something like that.

I will give you five reasons why Christians are sometimes cruel toward each other.

(1) They get to playing God and fall into judging each other.

(2) They forget that they themselves not only *were* sinners, but *are* sinners and always will be sinners, though saved by grace. They need to join the human race.

(3) They are still babes in Christ. Anger and raw hatred are often expressed by children. We need to be Christian Christians, if you get what I mean.

(4) They forget, if they ever knew, that the way to help people is not to attack them but to love them.

(5) Some of the so-called Christians have never been born again. They are like Mark Twain's man who "was a good man in the worst sense of the word."

Did I say "they"? "Fret not thyself because of evildoers." Just set them a better example.

Bad Disease Problem

QUESTION: *A family in our community is reported to have a bad disease. Their little girl has been riding to church with our family and playing with many of our children. The mother seems a little feeble-minded and it is hard for all of us to know how to treat them. Should we continue to pick up this girl or go a long way around in order to avoid passing their house?*

ANSWER: Consult your family physician, but I think your fears about the disease are largely unfounded. I judge you mean some venereal disease. (When will Christian people quit being falsely modest, and start calling a spade a dirty shovel?)

In the first place, I would be certain that this family has a venereal disease before I passed the word around. If there is any real evidence, the county health officer should be consulted to see that the case is cured. He might even be able to tell you how to handle the matter.

Whatever you do, try not to mistreat this little girl. Your Christian witness is at stake, and I should certainly hope that the church would do everything possible not to hinder her development. We owe something to such children. God loves the feeble-minded too.

You needn't be afraid of this case being identified. I get hundreds of such letters from a dozen different states.

Billy Graham Revivals

QUESTION: *What do you think of the Billy Graham revivals? Some of my fundamentalist friends say that he is neo-orthodox. Some of my liberal friends say that he is dividing modern churches and setting back our growth in fellowship between the churches. It seems to me that God is using Billy Graham in a mighty way.*

ANSWER: The way we use our terminology is sometimes a little sickening. We use labels like "liberal" and "fundamentalist" and then crucify those who happen not to agree with us.

I'll tell you what I think of Billy Graham. He is limited like any other man of God and makes mistakes. Some of his messages and methods are not what I would personally prefer. But I thank God for him and the marvelous way he is being used to present the basic Christian message to millions. I pray for him regularly and wish for him the best of God's blessings.

Why, every time a man gains a little fame, do we have to take pot-shots at him? We seem to be looking for something to divide over. May God help us to learn how to love, and to live together with those who may differ a bit from us.

Join the Human Race

QUESTION: *Recently you advised a person who never felt comfortable as a Christian to "join the human race." All my life I have felt something lacking in my life, and this statement seems to fit my case. Sometimes I feel I shall go insane trying to have the feeling of belonging to God. People don't know what goes on inside me. How do I increase my faith? There must be a defect in my character somewhere, and at my age (fifty-six) this bothers me.*

ANSWER: Really, I feel very sorry for you. I meet so many people who suffer from this "tyranny of the should" as one writer calls it. Even many Christians encourage this kind of unhappiness. They seem to think that if they feel bad about themselves, they will act better to their neighbor. The exact opposite is true.

Look at yourself. Does punishing yourself by self-reproach make you a better person? Why do you hate yourself? You do not know, do you? Then the only thing for you to do is to remember that God knows all about your inner loneliness and stays closer to you than the artery in your neck. Use what little faith you have. This is what Jesus said to some disciples who asked for an increase of faith (Lu.17:5–6).

By joining the human race, I mean accept your limitations. Quit trying to sit in God's lap. And stop trying to fly—angels fly. Acknowledge that you are a sinner and always will be, and see what God's power can make of you. "Consider the lilies of the field how they grow" (Matt. 6:28f.).

᥉ INDEX

actors, 78
Alcoholics Anonymous, 10, 11
alcoholism, 10, 11
allergies, 13
anger (*see also* quarreling), 16,
  28, 34, 35, 49
anonymous letters, 132
anxiety, 13

bad temper, *see* anger
Bertocci, Peter A., 107
Bible, versions of, 48, 117-118

capital punishment, 89
chain letters, 83
children:
  disciplining of, 58, 59, 88
  wayward, 54, 60, 70
choir members, 119
choosing a mate, 65, 67, 68,
  71-72, 74-75, 77, 96
Christian lawsuits, 90-91
Christian Sabbath, 84-85
Christmas, 126-127
church problems, 109-132
Clinebell, Howard J., 10
cliques in church, 131
college, women's, 69
confession, 138-139
conscience, 15, 18, 19, 42, 136-
  137
contributions, 113-114

conversion, 134-135
counseling, 19, 24, 38, 39, 41,
  42, 68, 88, 122
criticism, 8, 20, 28, 35, 60, 107,
  133-134, 139, 141, 143

dating, 69
death:
  and children, 58
  condition after, 98, 99, 102
  fear of, 18, 19
  of infants, 18-19, 99
  wish for, 3, 18-19
debts, 91, 118
deformity, 121
depression:
  anger in, 3
  cure of, 15, 21, 42
dictator, 113-114, 116, 123, 124
disease, spreading of, 42
divine healing, 14
divorce, 23, 24, 27, 29, 32, 33,
  34, 39, 45, 72, 82-83, 87, 95
doctors, 5, 35, 142
dominating parent, 62, 73
dominating wife, 37
doubt, 103-104, 136-137
dress, 79, 80, 104-105
drinking (*see also* alcoholism),
  5, 75, 86

Earle, Clifford J., 10

elderly people, 8, 115
enemies, loving, 97, 135-136
evolution, 106-107

faith, 14, 17, 103, 136-137
faith healing, 14
family altar, 63
family problems, 50-64
fear, 17, 20, 58, 62, 125
forgiveness, 21, 30, 42, 44, 45,
    46, 76, 95, 135-136

God's call, answering, 137-138
Graham, Billy, 143
grief situations (see also worry),
    6, 7
growth, 58, 60, 73, 109-110,
    121, 123
guilt feelings, see worry

Hamites, 81-82
hate, 50, 56, 57
heathen, state of, 102
homosexuality, 61
honesty, 2, 60, 62, 138
hostility, 27, 28, 34, 35, 42, 55,
    57, 62, 135-136
How to Help an Alcoholic, 10
human race, joining the, 56,
    144
husband, obedience of wife to,
    47, 48
husband-wife problems, 26-49,
    64

illegitimacy, 54, 70
infidelity, see unfaithfulness
in-laws, 25, 50-53, 56
Introduction to the Philosophy
    of Religion, 107

jealously, 41
Jews, 108

lawsuits, 91

lonely-hearts club, 66, 74
love, 37, 65, 67, 68, 71-72, 74,
    76-77, 91, 97, 124
loveless marriages, 23, 24, 27,
    29, 30, 31, 33, 36, 38, 39,
    43
loving enemies, 97, 135-136

Mann, Marty, 10
marriage, 65, 67, 68, 71-73, 77,
    122
married person, in love with,
    66
mental illness, 1, 2, 4, 6, 8, 9,
    28, 87-88, 132
Methodist Church, 40
middle-age (see also elderly
    people), 27, 29-30, 64
mother-daughter relationships,
    57, 73-74
mother-in-law problems, 50-54,
    56
motion pictures, 85-86
mourning, 6, 7

name, first, use of, 120
neglect of family, 26-27
Negro, see race problems

obedience of wife, 47, 48
older people, 8, 115

parents, 21, 25, 54
    dominating, 62, 73
pastor, 33, 72-73, 90-91, 94, 116,
    118, 122, 137-138
phobias, 17
picture shows, 85-86
play, 4, 93-94, 128-129
positive thinking, 13, 14
prayer, 4, 17, 20, 23, 26, 27, 30,
    31, 32, 35, 41, 60, 63, 64,
    70, 110, 124, 135-136
Primer on Alcoholism, 10

psychiatrists, 1, 18-19, 41, 61, 68, 87-88
psychopathic personality, 4, 66
psychotherapy, 18, 19, 61, 68
punctuality, 23

quarreling, 16, 28, 34, 49, 55, 57

race problems, 81-82, 90-91
recreation at church, 93, 94, 128, 129
remarriage, 72, 73, 82
repentance, 44, 103
revenge, 44, 89
Revised Standard Version of Bible, 48, 117-118
Rosenwald, Julius, 29

Sabbath, 84
salvation, 98, 99, 102, 103
self-esteem, 8
selfishness, 40
self-punishment, 42, 144
sermon titles, 130
sex (see also unfaithfulness), 54, 61, 70, 76, 138-139, 140
shock treatments, 5
sins, 1, 5, 15, 44, 54, 70, 76, 100-102, 133-134, 138-139, 140

sisters quarreling, 57
slighting of people, 114-116
slovenliness, 112-113
spinsters, 65, 74-75
sports at church, 93
stealing, 59, 109-110
suffering, 101
suicide, 1, 105-106
Sunday, 84

teen-age problems, 60, 70, 79-81, 104-105
temper, 16-17, 34, 35
temptation, 45, 140
thoughts, judgment for, 139
tithing, 110-111, 113-114
treasurer, 124

Understanding and Counseling the Alcoholic, 10
unfaithfulness, 29-31, 33, 40, 42, 44, 45, 64
unpardonable sin, 100

wife, obedience of, 47, 48
women in church, 111-112
women's colleges, 69
worry (see also grief situations), 12, 15, 18-19, 21, 22

Index of Scripture Passages

OLD TESTAMENT

Genesis:
9:18-29, 81
Deuteronomy:
22:5, 104
II Samuel:
12:23, 99
Psalms:
73, 101
103:12, 95

Jeremiah:
5, 101

NEW TESTAMENT

Matthew:
5:22, 17
5:25-26, 89
5:48, 51
6:28f., 144

Matthew (*continued*)
  10:32, 103
  17:20, 83
  19:17, 51
  21:12-13, 93
  21:43, 108
Mark:
  2:23-28, 83
  3:5, 17
  11:15-17, 93
Luke:
  12:5, 20
  13, 101
  17:5-6, 144
  19:45-46, 93
  23:43, 98
  23:46, 98
John:
  1:12, 136
  2:14-16, 93
  3:16, 106, 136
  5:24, 106
  7:17, 136
  9, 101
  10:27-30, 100, 106
  13:34-35, 103
  14:21-24, 103
  17:15, 96
Acts:
  4:12, 102
  7:59, 98
  9:17, 120
  10:34-35, 108
  17:26, 81-82
Romans:
  1:20, 102
  1:26-27, 61
  8:9, 103
  10:9, 103, 136
  13:1-4, 89
  14:21, 86
I Corinthians:
  6:14, 96

  11:19, 131
  13:11, 17
  14:34-35, 111
  15:51f., 98
II Corinthians:
  5:7, 137
  5:8, 98
Galatians:
  3:28-29, 108, 111
Ephesians:
  4:26, 17, 55
  5:21-33, 47
Philippians:
  1:23, 98
Colossians:
  3:18, 47
I Thessalonians:
  4:13-18, 98
I Timothy:
  2:9, 104
  2:10, 111
  2:12-15, 111
Titus:
  2:5, 48
  3:10-11, 131
Hebrews:
  4:15, 140
  10:17, 95
James:
  1:14, 140
I Peter:
  1:3-5, 100
  2:23, 89
  3:1-6, 48, 104
I John:
  1:7, 106, 138
  1:8-10, 51, 56
  2:3, 103, 136
  2:15, 85
  3:14, 103
  3:20, 136
  3:24, 136
  5:10-13, 103, 136